Two Kinds Of Christians

Which One Are You?

JOSEPH CHARLES BEACH

TWO KINDS OF CHRISTIANS

Which One Are You?

JOSEPH CHARLES BEACH

For permission requests and ordering information
Joseph Charles Beach
617 Sweet Gum Drive
Euless, TX. 76039
https://forgivenbyfaith.com
817-905-1956

Because of the dynamic nature of the Internet, any web addresses or links contained in this book may have changed since publication and may no longer be valid.

TABLE OF CONTENTS

INTRODUCTION

"Not everyone who says to me, 'Lord, Lord,' will enter the kingdom of heaven, but only the one who does the will of my Father who is in heaven. Many will say to me on that day, 'Lord, Lord, did we not prophesy in your name and in your name drive out demons and, in your name, perform many miracles?' Then I will tell them plainly, 'I never knew you. Away from me, you evildoers!'

Matthew 7:21-23

Nothing like starting off with such a positive message, right!

Matthew 7:21-23 is one of the most alarming passages in the entire Bible. It warns that not everyone who claims that Jesus is their Lord and Savior are actually saved. Here some *think* they know Christ, but will come to find out that Jesus never knew them!

This verse focuses on two groups, the true believer and the false believer, suggesting that there are two kinds of Christians.

We start here at Jesus' warning only because God loves and cares for us, and sometimes warnings are necessary. In Jesus day, just like today, there were many people proclaiming to be followers and believers. However, some are not on the right path according to Jesus. The warning was necessary to get their attention. There was still time to get things right for those who heard Jesus' words two-thousand years ago as well as today. If that were not true, then why would Jesus issue this warning?

Let me assure you the purpose for this book is not to be negative or judgmental. There will be far more positive words than negative. But to think you are really a true Christian but not really being on the right path is too important not to bring up. We must have the courage to truly examine ourselves, our attitudes, our actions, and our beliefs in light of scripture so we can be absolutely assured of our final destination.

I hear many pastors proclaim how easy it is to be saved. Perhaps this is true but to be honest I'm not really even sure what they mean when they say this? Are they talking about the process of saying a magical prayer, or being sincere when saying this prayer, or are they saying living a Christian life is easy? The important thing is, how do we really know that we are saved and how do we truly know Jesus and how does He truly know us?

Are we deceived into thinking we are saved when we are actually condemned and cast away from Jesus? Jesus goes so far as to actually call these people evildoers! Does this concern you? It should concern all of us.

If you're not concerned then you can stop reading. There is no point in going forward. But...if this concerns you, if you want to know for sure that you are saved or want to know how to be saved, then keep on reading.

It's not too late?! Jesus gives us this warning to get us on track. After all, would Jesus speak these words if it were too late? We all know we are not perfect, and that's okay. We know someone who is and that's our focus. We should never take our eyes off Jesus.

We must realize that no one is perfect. The goal is not to be perfect; the goal is that we must be sincere. Look again at the scripture. Matthew 7:21-23 says to enter the kingdom of heaven we must do the will of the Father in heaven.

The question is, how do we do the will of our Father?

I believe we must start with self-evaluation. We must evaluate ourselves on a daily basis. We are living in an un-Godly culture in this world. It's easy to be sucked in to this culture and become suffocated in it without even a notice. We trade the priorities of God in for the priorities of the world.

To do the Fathers will we must love God above all things. More than our culture, our political party our family and our friends.

God comes first, not just some of the time but *every* time! God and nothing else is our first and top priority!

We must also obey God and his word. We must read and meditate on his word, the Bible, and live according to God's word.

"And if you faithfully obey the voice of the Lord your God, being careful to do all his commandments that I command you today, the Lord your God will set you high above all the nations of the earth.
Deuteronomy 28:1

This also means we must learn to surrender our personal desires and focus on what God desires. When we surrender to God, we place his desires above our own. We live for Christ and not for ourselves. In loving God and people, we become less self-focused and become others-focused.

The next thing we must do is to love people.

"Teacher, which is the great commandment in the Law?" And he said to him, "You shall love the Lord your God with all your heart and with all your soul and with all your mind. This is the great and first commandment. And a second is like it: You shall love your neighbor as yourself. On these two commandments depend all the Law and the Prophets."

Matthew 22:36-40

Next, we must save the lost. God loves the lost and so should we. In fact, this is why Jesus came to the earth.

For the Son of Man came to seek and to save the lost."

Luke 19:10

As we move forward, we will focus on how to shift our thinking and our priorities away from the world and focus on Jesus.

We will become real Christians when we reach this goal.

We must also know what it means to be a true Christian. Let's start by looking at some statements or definitions on what it truly means to be a Christian in the first place.

A Christian is a person who has, by faith, received and fully trusted in Jesus Christ as the only Savior from sin (John 3:16; Acts 16:31; Ephesians 2:8–9).

"I told you that you would die in your sins, for unless you believe that I am he you will die in your sins."

John 8:24

That person becomes a "new creation" in Christ (2 Corinthians 5:17), the Holy Spirit comes into that person's heart, soul, mind, and spirit to dwell there forever (Ephesians 3:17; 1 Corinthians 6:19; Romans 8:11), and that person has been redeemed by Christ.

This new creation does not live like the old person once did, as a slave to sin. He is now a slave to righteousness and sin no longer has a hold on him (Romans 6:16–18). Do Christians still sin? Yes. But we hate our sin and want to be rid of it. We don't live in a manner inconsistent with our faith in Christ.

"You, however, are not in the flesh but in the Spirit, if in fact the Spirit of God dwells in you. Anyone who does not have the Spirit of Christ does not belong to him."

Romans 8:9

We note that to be a Christian we must have the Spirit of Christ in us. If we don't have the Holy Spirit in us, are we really a Christian?

"Whoever is not with me is against me, and whoever does not gather with me scatters."

Matthew 12:30

As authentic Christians we must also recognize that Jesus is God and has come in the flesh.

"Beloved, do not believe every spirit, but test the spirits to see whether they are from God, for many false prophets have gone out into the world. By this you know the Spirit of God: every spirit that confesses that Jesus Christ has come in the flesh is from God."

1 John 4:1-2

For Christians the difference also lies in the authenticity of a person's actions. Some may profess to follow the teachings of Jesus, but their actions tell a different story.

We must be able to recognize that certain behaviors don't align with the principles of Christianity.

A clear sign that reveals truth is the inconsistency between our words and actions. We may preach about love and forgiveness, but our actions don't line up with our words. We might be quick to judge others, hold grudges, or lack empathy.

Observing this stark contradiction can be a clear indicator that we may be wearing a mask of Christianity but we lack its essence. The essence of Christianity, like any faith, lies in its genuine practice. It's about embodying the teachings, living by the principles and extending love and compassion to others.

Being a Christian isn't about checking off items on a list or pretending to be who we aren't. It's about the authenticity of one's actions and the sincerity of one's faith. Recognizing these behaviors can help us navigate our relationships and foster genuine connections based on shared values and mutual respect.

Being a Christian isn't our ability to recite scripture or to have a perfect church attendance. It's the love we radiate, the compassion we extend, and the humility we exhibit. As Jesus himself said;

"You will recognize them by their fruit."

Matthew 7:16

We must bear fruit, not just bear the leaves.

Some people today, just like in Jesus' day, sincerely believe they are genuine Christians because of something they have done, such as reciting a prayer, responding to an "altar call" or becoming baptized. These are all good things, but none of these traditions provide salvation in itself, our salvation only comes by what lives in our heart, our sincerity of fully accepting and living out the gospel of Jesus Christ and placing our faith only in Him.

Believing in Jesus is more than just knowing Jesus lived on the earth. Even the demons knew this. It's putting this belief into action and placing your faith in Jesus fully and completely. It's a heart and soul commitment to place Jesus in the center of our lives.

But someone will say, "You have faith and I have works." Show me your faith apart from your works, and I will show you my faith by my works. You believe that God is one; you do well. Even the demons believe—and shudder!"

James 2:18-19

Doing good works is important but in of itself isn't enough. Our faith should give us the desire to do good works but good works do not save us.

"We have all become like one who is unclean, and all our righteous deeds are like a polluted garment. We all fade like a leaf, and our iniquities, like the wind, take us away."

Isaiah 64:6

It is by faith we are saved. This faith gives us the righteousness of Jesus. Then good works will come. We must remember however that good works is a Godly term and not a worldly term. What I mean by this is that the definition of good works is totally different in the eyes of God and the eyes of the world. The world believes that you are doing good works whenever you help or assist someone. But with God, good works include one more dimension. The Christian definition of good works is doing something for the benefit of another human being(s) but always recognizing that God gets the credit and the glory, not the individual doing the good work. In the world a rich person can give a large sum of money to a hospital and have his name plastered on the building but in this case the individual receives the credit and the glory, not God. So, never brag about your good works and always give God the honor and the credit.

Beware of practicing your righteousness before other people in order to be seen by them, for then you will have no reward from your Father who is in heaven. "Thus, when you give to the needy, sound no trumpet before you, as the hypocrites do in the synagogues and in the streets, that they may be praised by others. Truly, I say to you, they have received their reward. But when you give to the needy, do not let your left hand know what your right hand is doing so that your giving may be in secret. And your Father who sees in secret will reward you.

Matthew 6:1-4

It's important to remember that no Christian is perfect. We all fall short. However, a true Christian doesn't live in a state of continual, unrepentant sin. The practice of sin is the mark of a non-Christian, not simply an immature Christian. As true believers mature in their faith, they will prove that they are new creations by their increasing love for God, continual repentance from sin, separation from the world, spiritual growth, and obedience to God's Word. [1]

During his ministry, Jesus encountered false believers often. And what did Jesus do? He warned them. Whether it was the Pharisees, who posed as righteous men of God, or large crowds, who posed as committed followers, Jesus constantly exposed counterfeits.

Sadly, many unauthentic Christians flaunt a self-righteous attitude or selfish behavior. To be fair, most Christians aren't intentionally false believers. They have either been handed a counterfeit Jesus or drifted away from the radical life Jesus calls his followers to follow.

It's entirely possible to be a perfect church attendee and be a long way from God. On the flip side, it's also entirely possible to be a sporadic church attendee and have an intimate relationship with God. Even though it's important to be in community with other Christians, it's time to drop the false idea that God values attendance more than people. People matter to God and they should matter to us. If not, this may be a cause for alarm. Unless we are able to love others, we will never be able to have a true understanding of what it means to be a Christian. Every human being on this earth is an image bearer of God. Every human being is part divine in nature. God created each individual with a plan and a purpose. We must be able to see what God has created in every individual. There is simply no room for hatred or self-superiority. We must love others because it is the very essence of our created being. Without this love for others, we are far away from God. We must make the choice to love others just as Jesus does. Make this a priority to learn to love others.

Years ago, I had a hard time loving others. My focus was always on my needs with little to no thought for the needs of others. At the stage of life where others were growing in love for others, I was still focused on myself. I had almost no love for others. I allowed bitterness and hatred to flourish in my life. I believed that I didn't need anyone else and my focus was in protecting myself even though my life became very lonely and unfulfilling. It took many years to overcome the delusion I was living in. Thankfully people entered my life who gave me the love I was searching for. These Christians lead me to loving God and others more sincerely. Once I started to learn about God and his love, I was able to lay down the hurt and bitterness I had been experiencing. It wasn't easy but over time I was able to realize that every individual is a product of a world gone awry. Every one of us has hurts and struggles in this world and we need others to help us overcome these issues. That's exactly why we must learn to have compassion for one another. It's almost impossible to overcome these issues on our own, but just one caring person can make a difference. We just need to make the decision to help someone else. When this happens, miracles happen. None of us would be capable of love without God sending in someone to help us. We didn't discover this on our own, it is only the work of God, using other broken people, to help us in our need.

"If anyone loves me, he will keep my word, and my Father will love him, and we will come to him and make our home with him. Whoever does not love me does not keep my words. And the word that you hear is not mine but the Father's who sent me."

John 14:23-24

Only true Christians can love Jesus and love others. Only God can give us a desire to love people and so we must set our efforts into learning as much as we can about God and his love. True Christians need to come to others and help them to see the love God has for them.

When we as Christians mature in our faith, we will exhibit more and more evidence of the love that God has given us and the capacity to give ourselves and our love to others. Love is how we become true Christians. It is the mark of a true believer. This is the nature of a true Christian. If you truly want to be a better Christian and learn to love others as yourself, please keep on reading. It's not as hard as you might think.

As we press in to Jesus, we will learn how to do the Father's will. We will focus not on our will but God's will. We will learn what we need to become true Chistian's and followers of Jesus. We will learn how to focus on others as much as we focus on ourselves and we will be able to accomplish loving others almost as much as we love ourselves. As we get started, let's put our focus on the right priorities in how we love God and prioritize God over everything in the world.

LOVING THE WORLD

"Do not love the world or the things in the world. If anyone loves the world, the love of the Father is not in him."

1 John 2:15

This may seem to be a confusing beginning after reading about how we are to love others in the previous section. What may be difficult in understanding is that the more we fall into the trap of loving the world, the more we actually fall into the trap of loving ourself and despising others. The world is very competitive and the world teaches us to look out for number one (ourselves). Loving the world turns into only being able to love ourselves and eliminate anything and anyone who gets in our way. Our country, as well as the entire world, is very divided. Even though the world seems to teach unity you must pay attention to the underlining message. Unity comes at a cost. It only comes when the world is able to eliminate everyone with a viewpoint contrary to the worlds. The world does in fact have a ruler.

"In their case the god of this world has blinded the minds of the unbelievers, to keep them from seeing the light of the gospel of the glory of Christ, who is the image of God."

2 Corinthians 4:4

We are told not to love the things of the world because if we do, the love of God is not in us.

"Do you not know that friendship with the world is enmity with God? Therefore, whoever wishes to be a friend of the world makes himself an enemy of God."

James 4:4

Many of us spend more time on the computer, watching TV, being on social media, or spending time on our hobbies, than we do in church, reading the Bible, or in prayer. It's not that these things are wrong, it's just that we focus on the wrong priorities. How we spend our time is a clear indication of where our heart is.

*For where your **treasure** is, there your heart will be also.*

Matthew 6:21

It's important that we learn to see the world like Jesus does, seeing the world through God's eyes.

"And do not be conformed to this world, but be transformed by the renewing of your mind, so that you may prove what the will of God is, that which is good and acceptable and perfect."

Romans 12:2

But doesn't God love the world?

"For God so loved the world that he gave his only Son, that whoever believes in him should not perish but have eternal life."

John 3:16

How do we wrap our heads around this apparent contradiction?

When the Bible says that God loves the world, it is referring to the human beings who live in the world, not the culture and values of the world. God loves people so should we.

"Beloved, let us love one another, for love is from God, and whoever loves has been born of God and knows God."

1 John 4:7

In the Bible, the term world can refer to the earth and physical universe, but it most often refers to the humanistic system that is at odds with God.

"If you were of the world, the world would love you as its own; but because you are not of the world, but I chose you out of the world, therefore the world hates you."

John 15:19

When we are told not to love the world, the Bible is referring to the world's corrupt value system. Satan is the god of this world, and he has his own value system contrary to God's.

"For all that is in the world—the desires of the flesh and the desires of the eyes and pride of life—is not from the Father but is from the world."

1 John 2:16

The world is what we leave when we come to Christ. Isaiah 55:7 says that coming to God involves a forsaking of our own ways and thoughts. John Bunyan, in his book The Pilgrim's Progress, pictures the believer's position as having "his eyes lift up to heaven," holding "the best of books" in his hand, and standing with "the world as cast behind him" (p. 34).

The world often applauds sin. Hollywood encourages us to envy sinners and to foolishly compare ourselves with the "beautiful people."

"Let not your heart envy sinners, but continue in the fear of the Lord all the day."

Proverbs 23:17

Often the popularity of celebrities is due to their ability to stir in us dissatisfaction with our own lives. Advertisers prey on our natural tendency to love this world, and most marketing campaigns appeal in some way to the lust of the eyes, the lust of the flesh, or the pride of life.

The world also represents our society and culture. What we learn from our culture is far different than what is taught in the Bible. To be an authentic Christian you **must obey** the teaching of God over any teaching of our society. That includes issues of abortion (the value life), sexual behavior (including homosexual behavior), transgender transformation, and so on. If you choose to believe in the values of society over the values God teaches in the Bible, then you are obviously not believing what a true Christian should believe. If this is you, then perhaps you need to return to Matthew 7:21-23 in the beginning of the introduction of this book. This must be taken seriously, because believing in the worldly values over Biblical values places you in the same condition as those whom Jesus said, *'I never knew you. Away from me, you evildoers!'*

This also goes for the values of your political party. What values are they representing? Voting for members of a political party that opposes Biblical values makes us just as guilty as those we vote for, no matter what the issue.

This is one area that many nonauthentic Christians fail into. They vote for the party with unbiblical values and see absolutely nothing wrong with it. They have been lured in to following cultural values instead of Godly values. If this is you, it is time to re-evaluate your beliefs. Why would you consider following any value system that opposes the values of God and the Bible? The world and our society is good at giving us a false definition of love. Be careful with their definition. Yes, we should love all people but are to love members of our own gender with brotherly love, not erotic love. Don't fall into the false definition of love.

We as Christians must also value the gift of life. Don't fall into the trap of "reproductive rights" or the rights of what you can do with your body. Our bodies belong to God, and we are to use our bodies to glorify God.

"I appeal to you therefore, brothers, by the mercies of God, to present your bodies as a living sacrifice, holy and acceptable to God, which is your spiritual worship."

Romans 12:1

Human life is more valuable than a person's so-called rights into killing a baby in the womb. The reality is abortion is not a humane activity. It is an activity that results in the death of a human being. The child in the womb is a human being not just a lump of tissue as our society proclaims.

"Before I formed you in the **womb** *I knew you, and before you were born, I consecrated you; I appointed you a prophet to the nations."*

Jeremiah 1:5

Even though a child is in the womb of the female, it is not the females body. There is an independent living human being inside the womb an it is wrong to kill another human being based on where it's location is.

If you value the convenience of killing a human being more than having a greater value of human life created in the image of God, you must re-examine this outlook. Do you really know Jesus? Jesus would never agree with you point of view and may not even know you as well.

"But whoever causes one of these little ones who believe in me to sin, it would be better for him to have a great millstone fastened around his neck and to be drowned in the depth of the sea."

Matthew 18:6

Causing someone to sin caries a harsh penalty. Just imagine how much greater a penalty it would be to kill a human being than it is to cause a human being to sin!

You may be angry with what is written here but the purpose is that you may see and know Christ. Remember that Jesus is always prepared to forgive. It is never too late to change your values and come to Jesus. He will **always** welcome you home no matter how far away you have been. Find life in Jesus today and experience His love and mercy.

The goal here is to become a truly authentic Christian and not to remain a false Christian. Do not believe the lies of the world any longer. Do you want to truly follow God, or do you want to follow the world?

Letting the mindset of the world sway you more than the values of the Bible provides a strong indication of how well you know God.

If you truly desire to be a Christian, you must closely examine your values and make any needed adjustment. The choice is completely up to you. God gives us all the freedom to make our choices so we must choose wisely because there are consequences to the values and choses we make.

If you continue to follow the culture, society and your ungodly political party, you are following the world and not God. Is that really what you want to do? God's teaching should take priority over **every** area of our lives. How could anyone consider themselves to be a Christian if they don't agree in Christian values? It's just not possible!

Please take the warning of Jesus seriously. Do you really want to take a chance of Jesus saying to you, *'I never knew you. Away from me, you evildoers!'*

I pray not! And so should you!

After all, loving the world means being devoted to the world's treasures, philosophies, and priorities. God tells His children to set their priorities according to His eternal value system. This is our first priority.

"But seek first the kingdom of God and his righteousness, and all these things will be added to you."

Matthew 6:33

The other problem with trying to follow both the world and its values and trying to follow God and his values is stated by Jesus;

"No one can serve two masters, for either he will hate the one and love the other, or he will be devoted to the one and despise the other. You cannot serve God and money."

Matthew 6:24

Jesus says you must make a choice, Him or the world. Which one are you going to choose?

When we enter God's family through faith in Christ, God gives us the ability to put behind us the values of this world.

"Therefore, if anyone is in Christ, he is a new creation. The old has passed away; behold, the new has come."

2 Corinthians 5:17

We become citizens of God's and our desires turn heavenward, and we begin to store up eternal treasure. We realize what is truly important is eternal and we stop loving the world.

To continue to love the world the way unbelievers do will cripple our spiritual growth and render us fruitless for God's kingdom. Jesus took this thought a step further when He said,

"Anyone who loves their life will lose it, while anyone who hates their life in this world will keep it for eternal life."

John 12:25

Not loving the world extends to our own lives as well. Jesus said if we love anything more than Him, we are not worthy of Him.

And whoever does not take his cross and follow me is not worthy of me."

Matthew 10:38

Are you worthy of Jesus?

Loving the world means putting your faith and trust in the evil system controlled by Satan that leads us away from worship of God. John Calvin said, "The human heart is an idol factory." We can make idols out of anything. Any passionate desire of our hearts that is not put there by God for His glory can become an idol (1 Corinthians 10:31). Loving the world is idolatry (1 Corinthians 10:7, 14). So, while we are commanded to love the people of the world, we are to be wary of anything that competes with God for our highest affections. 1

As Jesus clearly stated we must all make a choice. We must choose to love only one master. Do you choose the world or God?

The parable of the Good Samaritan makes it clear we cannot pick and choose whom to love.

Jesus replied, "A man was going down from Jerusalem to Jericho, and he fell among robbers, who stripped him and beat him and departed, leaving him half dead. Now by chance a priest was going down that road, and when he saw him, he passed by on the other side. So likewise, a Levite, when he came to the place and saw him, passed by on the other side. But a Samaritan, as he journeyed, came to where he was, and when he saw him, he had compassion. He went to him and bound up his wounds, pouring on oil and wine. Then he set him on his own animal and brought him to an inn and took care of him. And the next day he took out two denarii and gave them to the innkeeper, saying, 'Take care of him, and whatever more you spend, I will repay you when I come back.' Which of these three, do you think, proved to be a neighbor to the man who fell among the robbers?" He said, "The one who showed him mercy." And Jesus said to him, "You go, and do likewise."

Luke 10:30-37

This may have been a difficult chapter; in fact, I am sure there are some who became angry and have stopped reading. The topics we have covered can be very divisive and I am truly sorry if anyone is offended. My desire is only to provide the same warning that Jesus gave and to help people that truly desire a relationship with Jesus to truly know Jesus. We all probably know someone with these false worldly values. We need to be able to reach out to them in love and kindness rather than keeping them in the dark. It is important that we have the conviction to teach the truth father than to not be offensive and love someone into hell. Relationships can be difficult; I know this from experience. My dad and I do not agree on any of these topics so I can do the easy thing and keep quiet, knowing where his eternal destiny could lead or speak up and make him angry. The choice is mine but the final result is heaven or hell. Where do you want your friends and family to be in their eternal destination? Let's pray for all those who believe in the lies, asking God to intervene in their lives so they can come to know the truth and live in the presence of Jesus for all eternity!

LOVING GOD

"Be strong and courageous. Do not be afraid or terrified because of them, for the Lord your God goes with you; he will never leave you nor forsake you."

Deuteronomy 31:6

Authentic Christians know God loves them.

They recognize their sin and rebellion separates them from God. They know Jesus came to earth, died and came to life again to offer forgiveness. Christian believers have a personal relationship with God. Having a personal relationship with God begins the moment we realize our need for Him, admit we are sinners, and in faith receive Jesus Christ as our Lord and Savior. God, our heavenly Father, has always desired to be close to us, to have a relationship with us. Before Adam sinned in the Garden of Eden (Genesis chapter three), both he and Eve knew God on an intimate, personal level. They walked with Him in the garden and talked directly to Him. Due to the sin of man, we became separated and disconnected from God.

What many people do not know, realize, or even care about, is that Jesus gave us the most amazing gift—the opportunity to spend eternity with Him if we have faith and trust in Him.

"For the wages of sin is death, but the gift of God is eternal life in Christ Jesus our Lord."

Romans 6:23

God became a human being in the person of Jesus Christ to take on our sin, be killed, and then be raised to life again, proving his victory over sin and death.

"Therefore, there is now no condemnation for those who are in Christ Jesus."

Romans 8:1

If we accept this gift, we have become acceptable to God and can have a relationship with Him. True Christians have a personal relationship with God and include God in their daily lives. They pray to Him, read His word, and meditate on verses in an effort to get to know Him even better. Those who have a personal relationship with God pray for wisdom (James 1:5), which is one of the most valuable assets we could ever have. They take their requests to Him, asking in Jesus' name (John 15:16). Jesus is the one who loves us enough to give His life for us (Romans 5:8), and He is the one who bridged the gap between us and the Father.

The Holy Spirit has been given to us as our Counselor.

"If you love me, you will obey what I command. And I will ask the Father, and he will give you another Counselor to be with you forever—the Spirit of truth. The world cannot accept him, because it neither sees him nor knows him. But you know him, for he lives with you and will be in you."

John 14:15-17

After Jesus gave His life and returned to heaven, the Holy Spirit became available to all who earnestly seek to receive Him. He is the one who lives in the hearts of believers and never leaves. He counsels us, teaches us truths, and changes our hearts. Without this divine Holy Spirit, we would not have the ability to fight against evil and temptations. But since we do have Him, we begin to produce the fruit that comes from allowing the Spirit to control us including: love, joy, peace, patience, kindness, goodness, faithfulness, gentleness, and self-control (Galatians 5:22-23).

This personal relationship with God is not as hard to find as we might think, and there is no mysterious formula for getting it. As soon as we become children of God (proclaim our faith in Jesus), we receive the Holy Spirit, who will begin to work on our hearts. We should pray without ceasing, read the Bible, join a Bible-believing church, and become involved in a small group of believers that gather on a regular basis. All these things will help us to grow spiritually. Christians take this seriously and make it a priority to put God first. If these are not part of your routine, then you may not be living the true Christian life that God desires you to be living.

Trusting in God to get us through each day and believing that He is our sustainer is the way to have a relationship with Him. Although we may not see changes immediately, we will begin to see change over time, and all the truths will become clear.

Any profession of faith that does not result in a changed life and good works is a false profession, and the person making the profession may not be a true Christian.

"Examine yourselves, to see whether you are in the faith. Test yourselves. Or do you not realize this about yourselves, that Jesus Christ is in you? —unless indeed you fail to meet the test!"
2 Corinthians 13:5

Paul instructed us to examine ourselves. A careful self-examination is certainly called for. The apostle Paul instructed those in Corinth to do this very thing.

"The ear that listens to life-giving reproof will dwell among the wise. Whoever ignores instruction despises himself, but he who listens to reproof gains intelligence. The fear of the Lord is instruction in wisdom, and humility comes before honor."

Proverbs 15:31-33

Do not be confused by this term "fear of the Lord." This term does not suggest that we should be afraid of God, it merely points to the fact that we should be in awe of God, having the highest respect and esteem for Him.

But what does it mean to examine ourself?

First, we do a "heart check." Are our hearts in the right spot? Are we divided among ourselves or unified in Christ?

Are we following God's Word and sinning less? Are there any unconfessed sins or un-surrendered areas in your life? Performing a "heart check" is to compare our values and beliefs to those of God in the Bible. It does not imply perfection but that we are growing in the right direction as we become more mature Christians. Paul wrote in 1 Corinthians 11:31–32 that we are to judge ourselves appropriately and allow the Lord to discipline and sanctify us. We should have the psalmist's attitude when he prayed, "Forgive my hidden faults" (Psalm 19:12).

Are we actually walking out our faith and living in active relationship with God, allowing Him to do His sanctifying work in our lives? Self-examination is an important part of living as an authentic Christian, but by nature we prefer self-deception. Deceiving ourselves is easy and comfortable. We want to believe ourselves better, smarter, and more ethical than we really are, so careful, spirit-directed self-examination keeps us honest with ourselves and with God.

We need self-examination to combat the spiritual deception rampant in the world. Scripture tells us to confess our sin to God, which requires a certain amount of self-examination. If we can never find any sin to confess, then "we deceive ourselves and the truth is not in us" (1 John 1:8). It is dangerous to lie to ourselves. Second

Corinthians 13:5 instructs us to examine ourselves to see if we are truly in Christ. One of Satan's favorite traps is to whisper false assurance to an unregenerate heart. Without spirit-directed self-examination, our enemy's lie becomes believable, and we deceive ourselves. One difficulty with self-examination is that we do not always know our own hearts.

"The heart is deceitful above all things, and desperately sick; who can understand it?"

Jeremiah 17:9

True self-examination must be done with the Holy Spirit, who searches the deep things of the heart (1 Corinthians 2:10–11). The church of Laodicea was in sore need of self-examination, but they had a hard time seeing their problem:

"For you say, I am rich, I have prospered, and I need nothing, not realizing that you are wretched, pitiable, poor, blind, and naked."

Revelation 3:17

The psalmist says;

"Search me, O God, and know my heart; Try me and know my anxious thoughts; And see if there be any hurtful way in me, and lead me in the everlasting way."

Psalm 139:23–24

The psalmist here admits that he does not even know whether his actions and motives are pure. So, he invites the Lord, the Righteous Judge, to test him and reveal to him his own sin.

Lack of self-examination can lead to ongoing self-deception; however, an over-attention to one's self is also unhealthy. We can become so inwardly focused that we take our eyes off of Jesus and make self-improvement our god. A.W. Tozer, in his classic work The Pursuit of God, says, "The man who has struggled to purify himself and has had nothing but repeated failures will experience real relief when he stops tinkering with his soul and looks away to the perfect One. While he looks at Christ, the very thing he has so long been trying to do will be getting done within him" (p. 85). We should examine ourselves in light of the truth being revealed to us from scripture and allow God's Word to convict and change us. At the same time, we must humbly admit our inability to change ourselves and rely on the power of the Holy Spirit within to transform us into the image of Christ (Romans 8:29). 1

The authentic Christian is satisfied with Jesus? Are you?

Do you have enough faith?"

This question reflects the doubt that most of us experience from time to time. And it's an honest question because who among us would say, "My faith is strong all the time"? We should never think this way because even the strongest faith can produce doubt from time to time.

If you look within yourself, you will always be disappointed because your faith will almost always seem like it isn't enough. If you look at your heart, you will see your own sinfulness. If you look at your outward performance, you will be discouraged by your failure to live like a true Christian. An honest self-examination leads to this conclusion: We have done those things we ought not to have done. We have left undone those things we ought to have done.

Either way you look at it, we're all miserable failures, pathetic losers in the great game of life, and if God only wants winners in heaven, then we're never going to make it because all have sinned and fallen short of the glory of God.

Don't look to yourself to find the answers because you will only be disappointed. You have to look outside yourself. That means looking to Jesus.

When we look to the Lord, this is what we find. Two thousand years ago Jesus died on the cross, shedding his blood for our sins. He died in our place, bearing our sins, taking our punishment, that we might be saved, cleansed, forgiven, declared righteous, be born again and become the true children of God. When God looked down from heaven and saw Jesus dying there, He said, "I am satisfied with what my Son has done." We know He was satisfied because on the third day, He raised Jesus from the dead.

God is satisfied with what his Son has done. Are you?

That's the central question of the spiritual life. Are you satisfied with Jesus? Or do you think that you need to add something to what He did for you?

An authentic Christian is a person who is truly satisfied with Jesus and what He did on the cross. A real Christian is someone who is so satisfied with Jesus when He says, "I am trusting the Lord Jesus Christ completely for my salvation."

Upon a life I did not live, upon a death I did not die, I stake my whole eternity on Jesus.

Are you satisfied with Jesus? Look to Him for your salvation. Trust Him completely. Place all that you are in his hands and say, "Lord, I'm coming to you as my Lord and Savior." It's as simple and as profound as that.

An authentic Christian takes the following actions:

1.) We admit.

I admit that without Christ I can do nothing. John 15:5 says, *"I am the vine; you are the branches. Whoever abides in me and I in him, he it is that bears much fruit, for apart from me you can do nothing."* Admit that. Simple say that and believe that. We are helpless to do anything of any significance, any eternal value, any spiritual worth whatsoever in any way without Christ.

2.) We Pray

I pray. If you admit you can do nothing, you say, "O God, help me." *"Ask, and you will receive,"* Jesus said (John 16:24). *"You do not have, because you do not ask"* (James 4:2). *"Call upon me in the day of trouble"* (Psalm 50:15). So, ask the Lord for freedom from self-consciousness. Ask for authentic emotion, and ask for protection from error, and ask for a prophetic anointing so that our words can miraculously penetrate and liberate others. If we truly want this, we must ask the Holy Spirit for it.

3.) We Trust

Trust for a specific promise. Trust for any situation that is needed in your life. Trust that God can do anything through you. Don't just in general, trust that He promised to do something for others through you. We are helpless to do anything of any significance, any eternal value, any spiritual worth whatsoever without Christ. *"It is not you who speak, but the Holy Spirit who speaks through you"* (Matthew 10:20). Trust in the promise and put your faith in it.

4.) We Act

Act in obedience to God's word, expecting God to act in and through us. So, act. *"Work out your own salvation with fear and trembling."* (Philippians 2:12). *"By the Spirit . . . put to death the deeds of the body"* (Romans 8:13). We are the actor and God is the miracle-maker.

5.) We Thank

And then, finally, when you are done, sit down and thank God. Thank God for whatever good comes. Thank Him and give Him glory. *"Give thanks always and for everything to God the Father in the name of our Lord Jesus Christ."*

Ephesians 5:20.

A true Christian will always put their trust in God and not in themselves. This is what it means to live by the Spirit, and walk in faith by the Spirit, and work out our salvation, and act the miracle of the Christian life. 2

Authentic Christians live with gratitude to God.

Living a life full of gratitude to God is what makes an individual an authentic Christian.

Obedience to God's law is an opportunity to thank Him for His blessings. This obedience isn't about seeking God's approval but showing Him love and appreciation.

Gratitude frees us from constantly worrying about our performance as Christians. Instead of focusing on becoming good enough, gratitude helps express joy in serving God. A life lived with gratitude is considered an opportunity to serve the Lord. Authentic Christians, being the followers of Christ, should show gratitude to God by worshipping Him, reading the Bible, interacting with neighbors, and performing well at their jobs.

Moreover, we should be bearing witness to our faith and using our leisure time by participating in community growth. If anyone lacks self-reflection, it is a sign of not being an authentic Christian.

Christianity encourages introspection and self-reflection, urging its followers to constantly evaluate and better themselves. Unbelievers often lacks this trait. They are quick to point out the mistakes of others but fail to reflect on their own shortcomings. They're resistant to change, often hiding behind their religious facade to avoid confronting their own flaws.

An authentic Christian understands that self-reflection is a crucial part of personal and spiritual growth. We are open to change and constantly strive to improve ourselves based on the principles of our faith.

Authentic Christians have a spiritual relationship with God by developing friendship with Jesus Christ and knowing Him. It is indeed the doorway to getting closer to God and to love God. A follower must commit to following Jesus to discover their relationship with God.

Doubts about our salvation can be troubling, but false assurances can be worse. Thankfully, we have scripture as our guide. There are specific things we can look for when determining the validity of our faith: trust in Christ, obedience to His Word, the presence of the Holy Spirit, love for God's people, and continued spiritual growth. We don't need to live in doubt. When Jesus is Lord of our lives and we live to please and honor Him, we can know beyond a doubt that we are true Christians (Matthew 6:33; Luke 6:46; John 14:15).

Authentic Christians have a hungering and thirsting for God.
Most Christians love to learn and they feel a strong need to read the Bible. To hunger and thirst for this is a strong indicator that the Holy Spirit is actively working in a believer. In the Beatitudes, Jesus said, *"Blessed are those who hunger and thirst for righteousness, for they will be filled"* (Matthew 5:6). David had this intense hunger and thirst, writing;

"O God, you are my God, earnestly I seek you; my soul thirsts for you, my body longs for you, in a dry and weary land where there is no water."

Psalm 63:1

"Come, all you who are thirsty, come to the waters; and you who have no money, come, buy and eat! Come, buy wine and milk without money and without cost."

Isaiah 55:1

Only Jesus can satisfy this deep thirst, as He said;

"But whoever drinks the water I give him will never thirst. Indeed, the water I give him will become in him a spring of water welling up to eternal life."

John 4:14

An authentic Christian is one who is led and encouraged by the Spirit. Romans 8:16 says, *"The Spirit himself testifies with our spirit that we are God's children."* When we surrender our lives to Jesus, His Holy Spirit comes to indwell us and changes the way we view the world, ourselves, and God. He brings an understanding of spiritual truths we could never before grasp (John 14:26). He helps us commune with the Father when we don't know how to pray (Romans 8:26). He comforts us by bringing to mind the promises of God. He gives us a knowing that quiets our hearts when doubts arise. Romans 8:14 says that "as many as are led by the Spirit of God, these are the children of God."

An authentic Christian has confidence of his or her adoption into God's family because of the testimony of the Holy Spirit (Romans 8:15).

In order to have a healthy vertical relationship – intimacy and fellowship with God, you must first maintain your horizontal relationships with others!

We talk about the Lord. Notice what Moses said about this in Deuteronomy 6:7. *"You shall teach them diligently to your children, and shall talk of them when you sit in your house, and when you walk by the way, and when you lie down, and when you rise."*

Do you have a spouse or children that you love deeply? Then chances are that you want to spend time with them and talk with them. The same is true about our spiritual lives. If we have no desire to spend time with, or talk with the Lord, then something is amiss in our spiritual condition.

An authentic Christian loves the scriptures. Moses wrote in Deuteronomy 32:47 about the place that scripture should have in our lives. Scripture, speaking of itself, says, *"This is not an idle word for you. Indeed, it is your life."* Jesus reiterated this when He said,

"If anyone loves me, he will keep my word…whoever does not love me does not keep my words"

John 14:23-24

The Old Testament also proclaims;

"These words that I command you today shall be on your heart."

Deuteronomy 6:6

An authentic Christian wants to surround themselves with things of the Lord.

"You shall bind them as a sign on your hand, and they shall be as frontlets between your eyes. You shall write them on the doorposts of your house and on your gates."

Deuteronomy 6:8-9

There are different ways we can express this desire. Some of us decorate our homes with artistic expressions of scripture. Some fill their bookshelves with Christian books that build them up spiritually. Think about your wallet or purse or your smartphone. Do you keep pictures of people in these that are precious to you? When we surround ourselves with things that remind us of the Lord or of scripture, we are expressing the desire to be with the Lord in some capacity. If the outward expressions of your heart do not include things of the Lord, then something may be wrong.

Do you overestimate yourself? If you have an attitude that you are better than other Christians, you must stop and ask yourself why you think this way. An authentic Christian never over estimates themselves. They never think of themselves more highly than others.

"Do nothing from selfish ambition or conceit, but in humility count others more significant than yourselves. Let each of you look not only to his own interests, but also to the interests of others. Have this mind among yourselves, which is yours in Christ Jesus."

Philippians 2:3-5

"For by the grace given to me I say to everyone among you not to think of himself more highly than he ought to think, but to think with sober judgment, each according to the measure of faith that God has assigned."

Romans 12:3

Authentic Christians trust God to forgive their sins.

Jesus came to save all sinners and for us to repent of our sins. Authentic Christians have repented from their sins. The Hebrew word for repentance is 'Teshuvah' which also means to turn back. It's not important that we just confess our sins, we must turn away from our sins with a sincere desire that we do not want to do these sins any longer. It's not to say that we will not sin again because we will, but our love for God convinces us that we should not sin. The truth is we are all sinners, we are not perfect.

"For all have sinned and fall short of the glory of God."

Romans 3:23

In Luke Jesus said,

"Why do you call me good? No one is good except God alone."

Luke 18:19

Jesus' message is that no one does anything good enough to rescue themself from their sins and give them eternal life.

Do you admit you sin and are you repentant?

Are you sorry for your sins?

Only authentic Christians grieve their sins.

Authentic Christians know that Jesus died for us so that our sins can be forgiven and that because of Jesus' death on the cross and his resurrection from the dead, we can obtain everlasting life.

"For I delivered to you as of first importance what I also received: that Christ died for our sins in accordance with the Scriptures, that he was buried, that he was raised on the third day in accordance with the Scriptures."

1 Corinthians 15:3-4.

This verse tells us that a real Christian is someone who is believing that Jesus died for their sins, was crucified on the cross, died and was then resurrected. A real Christian believes these facts and has asked God to forgive their sins. Real Christians strive to submit to Christ in everything

"Submit yourselves therefore to God. Resist the devil, and he will flee from you."

James 4:7

An authentic Christian is Righteous

"Make sure no one deceives you; the one who practices righteousness is righteous, just as He is righteous; the one who practices sin is of the devil; for the devil has sinned from the beginning. The Son of God appeared for this purpose, to destroy the works of the devil."

1 John 3:7-8 (NASB)

Authentic Christians will sin less and less.

Christians do not want to sin and displease God. They will be striving to obey.

"For if you live according to the flesh you will die, but if by the Spirit you put to death the deeds of the body, you will live."

Romans 8:13

Authentic Christians have the mind of Christ.

"The natural person does not accept the things of the Spirit of God, for they are folly to him, and he is not able to understand them because they are spiritually discerned. The spiritual person judges all things, but is himself to be judged by no one. "For who has understood the mind of the Lord so as to instruct him?" But we have the mind of Christ."

1 Corinthians 2:14-16

An important test that must not be overlooked is that authentic Christians can read the Bible and understand it. Non-Christians cannot understand the Bible. That was Jesus' message in John 14:21.

Only authentic Christians can understand the Bible, because the Holy Spirit only helps Christians understand it. Sometimes a new Christian may have trouble understanding scripture because they are just starting to learn it. A mor mature Christian should be able to understand scripture when they study it. Yet, if the Christian has not been studying scripture as they should, then understanding may be more difficult. An authentic Christian is in the habit of reading the Bible and understand what the scriptures tell them. 3

A few more characteristics of authentic Christians are:

- The fruit of the Spirit is increasing in their lives.
- The Holy Spirit is living within them.
- The fruit of the Spirit will be becoming more obvious in them day after day.

Authentic Christians experience answered prayers.

"And whatever we ask we receive from him, because we keep his commandments and do what pleases him."

1 John 3:22

That is the key issue of the Christian life. That's the way Paul says he lived. And he means for us to live that way. He says;

"But by the grace of God I am what I am, and his grace toward me was not in vain. On the contrary, I worked harder than any of them, though it was not I, but the grace of God that is with me."

1 Corinthians 15:10

"How do we do that?" How do we work hard and yet be able to say that when I am done, "God's grace was the worker in and through me?" We do this by;

1.) Relying on the Holy Spirit and
2.) By obeying

"Therefore, my beloved, as you have always obeyed, so now, not only as in my presence but much more in my absence, work out your own salvation with fear and trembling, for it is God who works in you, both to will and to work for his good pleasure."

Philippians 2;12–13

How do we serve others in a strength that isn't your own?

"Whoever speaks, as one who speaks oracles of God; whoever serves, as one who serves by the strength that God supplies—in order that in everything God may be glorified through Jesus Christ. To him belong glory and dominion forever and ever. Amen."

1 Peter 4:11

How do you do that? By being an authentic Christian.

True Christians love the Lord

"If anyone has no love for the Lord, let him be accursed. Our Lord, come!"

1 Corinthians 16:22

If a person does not love Jesus, then they are divinely cursed.

Loving Christ is an important characteristic of any Christian. It tells us that a Christian is one who loves Christ. A Christian is also one who obeys Christ.

"And by this we know that we have come to know him, if we keep his commandments. Whoever says "I know him" but does not keep his commandments is a liar, and the truth is not in him."

1 John 2:3-4

Loving God is the first step of being a true Christian. Do you truly love God? Make it a habit to spend time with God, learning more about Him and His love for you. Become a lover of God. You cannot love someone if you do not want to spend time with them. Loving God and spending time with Him is the best way to realize how much God truly loves you.

So, what kind of Christian are you? Do love the world or God?

LOVING THE CHURCH

"Husbands, love your wives, as Christ loved the church and gave himself up for her."

Ephesians 5:25

A real Christian is one who displays a sincere love for the family of God. Although we should love all people, Christians naturally gravitate toward other believers. God's instructions are for us to grow in love by serving our brothers and sisters and helping them bear their burdens.

Our example of loving the church comes from Jesus. Jesus' love for the church is unconditional and sacrificial. Jesus' unconditional love for the church is a love that knows no bounds. It is a love that is freely given without expecting anything in return. Christ's love for the church goes beyond any conditions or requirements. His love is unwavering and all-encompassing, embracing every individual of the church, regardless of our flaws and shortcomings.

Christ's love for the church is sacrificial. He gave Himself up for her, laying down His own life as the ultimate act of love. This sacrificial love is a selfless love that puts the needs and well-being of others above one's own. Christ's sacrifice on the cross is a testament to the extent He was willing to go for the sake of His beloved church. This love provides us with the example of how we are to love the church. We must learn how we too can love fellow believers with an unconditional and sacrificial love.

Through Christ's unconditional and sacrificial love, we find reassurance that we are deeply valued and cherished. His love for the church knows no bounds. Let us attempt to mirror this love for fellow believers by extending love and grace to all those around us.

Christ is the head of the church. As the head of the church Jesus ensures the growth and well-being of the church, providing guidance and direction. His leadership is characterized by love, compassion, and a deep sense of responsibility. He takes on the role of a compassionate shepherd, caring for His flock.

Jesus as head of the church, has the final say in matters that concern the church, steering it in the direction that aligns with His divine plan. His leadership is rooted in love and wisdom, guaranteeing that the church remains united and focused on its mission.

"And he is the head of the body, the church. He is the beginning, the firstborn from the dead, that in everything he might be preeminent."

Colossians 1:18

What is the Church?

To be able to love the church like Jesus loves the church we must first understand what the church truly is. Paul's letter to the Ephesian church is probably the best answer to this question.

"So, then you are no longer strangers and aliens, but you are fellow citizens with the saints and members of the household of God, built on the foundation of the apostles and prophets, Christ Jesus himself being the cornerstone, in whom the whole structure, being joined together, grows into a holy temple in the Lord. In him you also are being built together into a dwelling place for God by the Spirit."

Ephesians 2:19–22

Paul goes on to say;

"For this reason I bow my knees before the Father, from whom every family in heaven and on earth is named, that according to the riches of his glory he may grant you to be strengthened with power through his Spirit in your inner being, so that Christ may dwell in your hearts through faith—that you, being rooted and grounded in love, may have strength to comprehend with all the saints what is the breadth and length and height and depth, and to know the love of Christ that surpasses knowledge, that you may be filled with all the fullness of God."

Ephesians 3:14-19

Paul says that all believers are the church. We're the church that God ordained from the foundation of the world. We're His people and our priority must be to support the church as best as we are able. As the church becomes the fellowship of all believers the church walks according to the power of the Holy Spirit. Then the people of God will shine as the light of the world. When people see that light, they will give glory to God (Matthew 5:16). When we love the church correctly, this will change the world. As the church, we must remember who we are, who the foundation is, who the cornerstone is, who the head of our building is, and who the Lord of the church is.

We, the church, have been made for this task by the indwelling presence and power of God's Spirit. Yet, we are called not so much to rise up but to bow down. And if we bow down to our Lord, our light will pierce the darkness. 1

In the book of Acts, the author writes that the members of the early church frequently gathered together;

"And they devoted themselves to the apostles' teaching and the fellowship, to the breaking of bread and the prayers."

Acts 2:42

Regular fellowship and community are therefore essential attributes of the church. No believer is intended to live out their faith alone. They have been given the Body of Christ for encouragement, strength, and support. This is why believers are called to spend time with other believers. It is also where the idea of Sunday morning or weekly "church" comes from.

The place where Christians gather to worship God and fellowship with each other bears the name of the church, however, the true purpose of the church exists beyond the building or place of worship. Its power is found in its people and their movement in the world.

"For just as the body is one and has many members, and all the members of the body, though many, are one body, so it is with Christ. For in one Spirit, we were all baptized into one body—Jews or Greeks, slaves or free—and all were made to drink of one Spirit."
1 Corinthians 12:12-13

As part of the Body of Christ, Christians are members of a much greater community.

"If one member suffers, all suffer together; if one member is honored, all rejoice together."
1 Corinthians 12:26

Each member of the "body" is valued.

Every individual member of the church, like each part of the human body, has a part to play in the spiritual Body of Christ. The church is at its strongest when everyone is contributing their individual talents and spiritual gifts to this community.

Each member of the "body" is imperfect.

Again, the Body of Christ is comprised of imperfect people who are constantly growing and will make mistakes. It is a God-anointed community made in the image of Christ that is nonetheless imperfect in its parts. That doesn't deny its effectiveness or purpose. The strength of the church all points to the unifying grace of God and power of His son Jesus Christ.

What is the Purpose of the Church?

The church is to proclaim the gospel to the world, equip Christians for ministry, and instruct it's members in God's word.

The church exists to train and equip its members for ministry, instruct its people in the teachings of Christ and scripture, and help believers grow closer to Jesus Christ and each other.

Jesus reminded His followers to be the "light of the world" and the "salt of the earth" (Matthew 5:13-16). As light, the church is called to represent the kingdom of God and be the living movement of Christ's love and grace in the world.

As Jesus said,

"Let your light shine before men in such a way that they may see your good works, and glorify your Father who is in heaven."
Matthew 5:16

The church's presence in the world should be the light that illuminates Christ's love for the world. As salt, the church is also called to be the moral and spiritual preservative of a broken world in need of healing. Christ's ministry was founded on healing the sick, caring for the poor, and freeing the oppressed from guilt, shame, and spiritual bondage. For the church to be effective, it must pursue this mission as well.

When the church is grounded in the grace of God and truth of His word, its members will be the love, joy, peace, patience, faithfulness, kindness, goodness, gentleness, and self-control the world desperately needs (Galatians 5:22-23).

To be a real Christian means we must support the Church!

The Church is not perfect, no Church is perfect. However, we are called to support the Church through thick and thin.

Because the church is made up of unperfect people, the church can fall short from time to time. Even when this happens, Jesus calls us to support the church through these difficult times. We are called to serve the church in the power of God the Holy Spirit. We don't leave the church when bad things happen, we come in to protect the church and fight for the church just as Jesus has done.

Unless the Church has turned away from teaching Biblical values, we must do all we can to lift up the Church even when things go wrong. The Church is the bride of Christ and we should take every effort to help and support the church when it goes through the valleys and the lows. If the church is there for us, we need to be there for the church. If you leave a church because a person, even a pastor, has committed a grievous sin, then we are guilty of following that person over the church. This is a clear indication that we are not authentic Christians. We must love the church the same way Jesus loves the church. Seeking the perfect church is a mission of futility, it will never be found. Even though we recognize that Jesus is the head of the church, we must remember that all churches are run by flawed human beings.

Stick it out. Don't assume the worst. Ask questions and seek answers. We are to be in prayer for our church and our church leaders. We are to step up and ask how we can help be part of the solution. Because churches are run by people, they can get messy. If you truly love the church like Jesus loves the church then be engaged.

Authentic Christians do not sit on the sidelines like observers, we are called to be players on the field. Get involved in church activities and volunteer where ever there is a need. Never assume there are enough volunteers because there never are. Jesus' church needs your help! Step up and take action.

Most Christians never volunteer in their church and they miss out on the blessings and fulfillment they can receive only by volunteering. Other people in the church need you. Volunteers are just as important to the church as the pastors and the elders. Step up in your commitment to the church, get involved, and serve.

When you support your church, you are supporting the ministry of God's kingdom here on earth. Never let the enemy tell you that you are not needed because that is a lie. The church needs you more than you can imagine. Authentic Christians always get involved and are never just spectators sitting on the sidelines. Now is your time. Get the blessing you deserve.

Maturing in your faith is important as you grow into the authentic Christian God has created you to become. Listen to God's calling. You are designed to do more than you can image. Take the first step in getting more involved with your church and sharing the gifts you were given with others who really need them. God calls us all to go first, then He will show us how to become the blessing we were designed to be to others.

Do you seek advice from God's people or only from God?

Many Christians fall into the trap of depending on God but not on God's people. Many unauthentic Christians develop and attitude that spending time with God will solve their problems and fill them with contentment but they don't see the same fulfillment being with God's people to fill this need. The truth is you need both. God works through his people!

Not relying on other believers for advice and support and growth is actually missing out on God's plan for your life. When you develop the attitude of staying home alone to be with God instead of meeting with other believers to share life together, you are actually failing to follow God's plan of fellowship and growth. This happens with well intending Christians because they inadvertently develop a "I am more spiritual" or "I am a more mature Christian" than everyone else and no one else can really help me because I have God and that's all I need!

If you have fallen into this trap wake up! God works through his people and through his church and He has no desire for you to be a "lone ranger" Christian. You must be an authentic Christian! You must fellowship with authentic Christians to gain the benefits that God has intended for you to have.

Yes, there is a time to spend with God alone in prayer and reading God's word. But when you fail to recognize the benefits of sharing life with other believers, you are only missing out on the blessings that God has in store for you.

Once you develop an attitude that you don't need any one but God, you have allowed pride to overtake your thinking and you are not walking the path that God created for you to follow.

As mentioned earlier, if you have an attitude that you don't need anyone else because you are so tight with God, then you may not be an authentic Christian. Unfortunately, many Christians fall into the trap of elevating themselves over others. What makes this so said is that often these are the people who need others the most. They refuse attending services with others thinking that spending time with God is more important. The truth is that spending time with God is important, but it is also important to spend time in fellowship with other believers. 2

"Then the Lord God said, "It is not good that the man should be alone."

Genesis 2:18

God's desire for your life is to spend time in fellowship with others. Take advantage of this fellowship. God works through other people. There are valuable lessons to be learned from others.

Do not be deceived in thinking that you don't need anyone but God. We all need others and it is God's will and desire for us to be in fellowship with others. Never think that you are superior to others in any way. If you continually brag about how much God talks to you then you do not have the spirit of an authentic Christian. This is especially true if there is no fruit in your life. If you are not actively serving others, yet God talks to you all the time, then why are you not serving others? What excuse do you have? That is an attitude of superiority and pride that is not pleasing to God, plus God commands us to serve others.

For we are his workmanship, created in Christ Jesus for good works, which God prepared beforehand, that we should walk in them.
Ephesians 2:10

Yes, God created us for the purpose of doing good works, which means to serve others. If you here God talking to you but He has never told you to serve, you must not be listening well enough. This is a clear sign of not being an authentic Christian!

"By this everyone will know that you are my disciples, if you love one another."
John 13:35

The church exists to strengthen and equip its members for an external relationship with a broken world. The church is a life-giving movement, alive and thriving in the power of God's grace and Christ's free gift of salvation to all. 3

How do we show our love and support for the Church?

1. Love the people of the church.
2. Love those not yet in the church.
3. Respond to the gospel message and share it.
4. Support the church always! (Good times and bad times).
5. Pray for the church.
6. Be involved in community with those in the church.
7. Depend on the Lord...and his people.

A real Christian is someone who regards Christ as infinitely more valuable than anything else, even earthly suffering.

"And you became imitators of us and of the Lord, for you received the word in much affliction, with the joy of the Holy Spirit."
1 Thessalonians 1:6

The Thessalonians responded to the gospel message and came to Christ from a background of idol worship. They faced enormous cultural pressure. No doubt some faced opposition from family members who thought they were nuts to believe in Jesus. In those early days of the Christian movement, it wasn't popular to be a "Christ-follower."

The Thessalonians were under pressure of being pushed down by those they knew. Still, they were able to receive the Word with joy. The Thessalonians were so glad to be saved they couldn't be stopped, not even by persecution.

Even today in many places in the world, being a Christian really costs something. Yet even in these situations, these Christians develop a much deeper joy than most of us who never face any persecution. Here we tend to take our blessings for granted. There every day is a gift from God, even in suffering.

Jesus never invites us to receive Him on a trial basis, although some try to do just that. In the words of Dietrich Bonhoeffer, "When Jesus calls a man, He bids him come and die." True conversion means that you continue to follow Christ even when the going gets rough.

A real Christian is changed by Jesus and is someone who joyfully chooses to follow Christ and his church no matter the cost. If you had to pay the price, would you?

Remember what Jesus said to the demon possessed man;

"Go home to your friends and tell them how much the Lord has done for you, and how he has had mercy on you."

Mark 5:19

The best place for you to make an impact for Christ is right where you are. Showing your friends and family God's love makes a huge impact. This will change the life of others.

Authentic Christians go "all in" on Jesus. We turn away from the things of the world and turn to God and serve the living and true God, and we wait for his Son in heaven knowing that Jesus delivers us.

There comes a moment when we have to decide to go "all in" about what we believe. This could mean risking everything but somewhere along the way you've got to make a stand.

Going "all in" for Jesus means we recognize that Jesus is the Son of God, that He died on the cross for our sins, that He rose from the dead on the third day, that He is the Lord of the universe. We can't go to heaven on our own, but only through Jesus. There is no other way. If you decide to go "all in" on Jesus, there is no plan B.

We must remember that it begins with God and his choice of us, it requires sharing the gospel with others, it leads to a heart-felt acceptance of Christ as Lord and Savior, it results in a changed life that changes other lives, and it means that we go "all in" on Jesus. It starts with God. It is based on truth of who Jesus really is. It changes everything about our lives.

Chose to be the right kind of Christian by loving the Church!

"We know that we have passed from death to life, because we love each other. Anyone who does not love remains in death."

1 John 3:14

LOVING OTHERS

Therefore encourage one another with these words.
1 Thessalonians 4:18

What is the link between God's love for us and our love for others? What converts the love of Christ for us into our love for others? The first answer is the Holy Spirit.

"For you were called to freedom, brothers. Only do not use your freedom as an opportunity for the flesh, but through love serve one another. For the whole law is fulfilled in one word: "You shall love your neighbor as yourself." But if you bite and devour one another, watch out that you are not consumed by one another."
Galatians 5:13–16

The Holy Spirit is the key. The fruit of the Spirit is love, joy, peace, patience, kindness, goodness, faithfulness, gentleness, self-control; against such things there is no law.

The first fruit of the Spirit listed here is love. It is plain that one crucial link between our being loved by Christ and our loving others is the Holy Spirit. Love for others is a fruit that grows in our lives by his doing. Somehow, He makes it happen. It won't happen without Him. And when it does happen, we don't get the glory for it, God does.

The Christian life of love is a supernatural life. It is not produced by merely human forces. It takes power and resources that we do not have. This is very crucial for us to admit. It is humbling. Left to ourselves we cannot love. We can only love because of the love God has given to us along with the influence of the Holy Spirit living in us. This is very encouraging because we do not have to rely on our own power to love others, the power is given to us as believers. I am not by nature a loving person, you are not at a disadvantage, because in fact, nobody is by nature a loving person. If we were, love would not be a fruit of the Holy Spirit; it would be a fruit of our personality or our upbringing or our chromosomes. In fact, you may be farther along than a person who feels that love is a natural thing. They will have a harder time learning how to love because they may not look for the correct source in the first place.

The Holy Spirit works in us in some supernatural way to bear the fruit of love.

Another ability necessary to love others is faith. There is a link between love and faith.

"For in Christ Jesus neither circumcision nor uncircumcision counts for anything, but only faith working through love."
Galatians 5:6

Faith works through love. We have the ability to love others by our faith. If you look to your own strength, or to the merit of the things you can do, then we will fail. When you depend on your works, you reject the work of Christ.

What connects us with Jesus so that the salvation He accomplished becomes ours is faith — trusting his forgiveness; banking on his promises; cherishing his fellowship. But what makes this so remarkable is that the faith that connects us with Jesus and receives his justification is "faith that works through love." In other words, it is a kind of faith that proves its reality by producing love. Love doesn't merit our salvation. Love proves the reality of the faith that receives salvation.

Paul answers the question by stating that "faith produces love." Faith is somehow a link between Christ's love for us and ours for each other. Then how do faith and the Spirit relate to each other in bringing about love?

Paul's answer is given again in Galatians,

"O foolish Galatians! Who has bewitched you? It was before your eyes that Jesus Christ was publicly portrayed as crucified. Let me ask you only this: Did you receive the Spirit by works of the law or by hearing with faith? Are you so foolish? Having begun by the Spirit, are you now being perfected by the flesh? Did you suffer so many things in vain—if indeed it was in vain? Does he who supplies the Spirit to you and works miracles among you do so by works of the law, or by hearing with faith."

Galatians 3:1–5

The Christian life is supposed to be lived every day in the same way that it began. In the Christian life you don't graduate from Spirit to flesh or from faith to works. The Christian life begins with faith and the Holy Spirit; and it is lived by faith and by the Spirit. Faith is the first grade of the Christian life and it is the graduate school of the Christian life. And the Holy Spirit is the teacher and the power at every level. We never graduate to something else. It's always faith and the Holy Spirit.

We have the Holy Spirit and faith brought together. What does it mean for us when we want to be a more loving people?

Paul says that at the beginning of the Christian life the Holy Spirit was received by faith, not works of the Law. The Spirit comes through the channel of faith. That's how we got started in the Christian life.

So, God is supplying or providing the Spirit to you in and ongoing way and working miracles among you in an ongoing way.   This happens by hearing with faith. The Holy Spirit is received the first time and is supplied for ongoing work in our lives not by works of law but by faith. The Spirit and faith relate this way: faith is the channel of the Holy Spirit. Love is the fruit of the Holy Spirit and the fruit of faith because faith is what receives and depends on the Holy Spirit. God supplies the Holy Spirit. He does this through faith. And love is the fruit of the Holy Spirit released or received by faith. The Holy Spirit is the sap that pours love into our lives; and faith is the root that we send down into the soil.

How Do We Become A More Loving People?

First, we experience more of the fruit of the Holy Spirit. We do this by believing and trusting in God. It involves a hearing of something to be trusted, something to be believed, something in which we have faith. Let the Holy Spirit fill your life with his power and fruit. Love is the fruit of the Holy Spirit. It is not the product of our hard work for God. It is fruit. God supplies the Spirit to us and works miracles among us (of which love is the greatest) by faith.

So, if you want to receive and release the Holy Spirit in his love-producing power, listen to the word and believe it, rest in it, bank on it, rely on it, and depend on it.

Make it your aim day and night to be filled with the fruit-bearing Holy Spirit. For the fruit of the Spirit is love. And to that end, make it your aim day and night to be filled with faith, trust, confidence in Christ. Make it your aim to be filled day and night with the word of God. 1

Our love for others is a witness to our identity as the redeemed sons and daughters of God. A church that is "missional," and wants to make Jesus known in their community, must be a church that loves others. And a church that is intentional about loving others can't help but be a church that makes Jesus known. That's the way it works.

And that's how we live together as the church in this world: we go against the grain of societies expectations, we help one another when it hurts, and we love one another to represent our King. 2

Our love for each other has great implications. Jesus says that "by this all people will know that you are my disciples, if you have love for one another." Why is it so hard, then, for us to love the way God calls us?

Our culture can use the word "love" in such a trivial way, but then the word "love" can also be used to refer to the deepest of relationships. No wonder it's so easy for us to miss the type of love God calls us to express toward, not just our favorite people, but toward all people.

So radical is the love that God commands us to have for others, it includes loving our enemies and persecutors.

"You have heard that it was said, 'You shall love your neighbor and hate your enemy.' But I say to you, love your enemies and pray for those who persecute you, so that you may be sons of your Father who is in heaven. For he makes his sun rise on the evil and on the good, and sends rain on the just and on the unjust. For if you love those who love you, what reward do you have? Do not even the tax collectors do the same? And if you greet only your brothers, what more are you doing than others? Do not even the Gentiles do the same? You therefore must be perfect, as your heavenly Father is perfect."

Matthew 5: 43-48

We must also love without expecting or receiving love back in return.

"But love your enemies, and do good, and lend, expecting nothing in return, and your reward will be great, and you will be sons of the 'Most High', for he is kind to the ungrateful and the evil. Be merciful, even as your Father is merciful."

Luke 6: 35-36

But the most challenging call to love is the great commandment:

"And he said to him, "You shall love the Lord your God with all your heart and with all your soul and with all your mind. This is the great and first commandment. And a second is like it: You shall love your neighbor as yourself. On these two commandments depend all the Law and the Prophets."

Matthew 22: 37-40

To truly love, we must first know God. Love starts with God and ends with God because God is love. We see this in First John:

"Beloved, let us love one another, for love is from God, and whoever loves has been born of God and knows God. Anyone who does not love does not know God, because God is love."

1 John 4: 7-8

Love is one of God's greatest attributes. All God does is out of love. He cannot and does not do wrong. His display of love is the purest and truest there is. He loves perfectly. And because we are made in God's image, we must love others.

For the kind of love that God calls us to–the love that loves our neighbor as much as we love ourselves– *that* must come from Him. We cannot love like that without first being born of God. God's common grace allows for all men made in His image to love, but there is a love that is set apart for the Christian. And it is also God's enabling Spirit that allows us to love God. We love God because He first loved us (1 John 4:19).

This command to love is important. God never says, "if you feel like loving, then love." Perhaps its most challenging because to display love in such a practical way causes even non-Christians to recognize that it's supernatural. We can't do it on our own. But with God, we can love radically:

"For the love of Christ controls us, because we have concluded this: that one has died for all, therefore all have died; and he died for all, that those who live might no longer live for themselves but for him who for their sake died and was raised."

2 Corinthians 5:14-15

Christ died so we might live for Him and we die to our flesh as we learn to love others. We have to move past how we feel about a situation or a person and ask God to give us a genuine love for others. This means putting others above ourselves. We'll know if we're sacrificially loving others because it's going to be a little painful. We may experience loss of time, sleep, money, energy, whatever it is, we will feel it. And that person who is being extended love will also know it.

Through the Scriptures, the Holy Spirit puts within the people of God a conviction to love people and make sure they know that they are loved. We fail miserably at this when we try to love in our own strength. We will never love God or anyone with our whole hearts. We fail at this because our flesh fights for us to be selfish and self-focused. Like Paul, when we want to do good, sin is right there with us (Romans 7:21). We may not always want to love, but we can choose to. Jesus loved perfectly in our place. And by God's grace, we will grow in loving others.

We must change our tendency of focusing on ourselves and neglecting others.

Christianity teaches us humility and respect for others' journeys. It's not about being better than others, but about becoming better versions of ourselves.

"If I speak in the tongues of men and of angels, but have not love, I am a noisy gong or a clanging cymbal. And if I have prophetic powers,

and understand all mysteries and all knowledge, and if I have all faith, so as to remove mountains, but have not love, I am nothing. If I give away all I have, and if I deliver up my body to be burned, but have not love, I gain nothing."

1 Corinthians 13:1-3

We know we are authentic Christians because we love other people. We desire their fellowship, and seek to serve them in deed and truth (1 John 2:7-11).

Surely a Christian cannot claim to be saved and yet hate people. The Apostle John gives evidence that a believer can know that they are born again.

Whoever says he is in the light and hates his brother is still in darkness. Whoever loves his brother abides in the light, and in him there is no cause for stumbling. But whoever hates his brother is in the darkness and walks in the darkness, and does not know where he is going, because the darkness has blinded his eyes.

1 John 2:9-11

No one can hate their brother or sister in Christ or any unbeliever and claim to be a follower of Jesus.

Jesus said that believers must love others. He raised the bar when He said;

"A new commandment I give to you, that you love one another: just as I have loved you, you also are to love one another. By this all people will know that you are my disciples, if you have love for one another."

John 13:34-35

If you love one another, this is how everyone, believers and non-believers, will know that we belong to Christ and anyone who is Christ's is safe and secure in knowing they are born-again.

Moses said in Leviticus 19:9, "Love your neighbor as yourself." The Apostle John took this even further.

"We love because he first loved us. If anyone says, "I love God," and hates his brother, he is a liar; for he who does not love his brother whom he has seen cannot love God whom he has not seen. And this commandment we have from him: whoever loves God must also love his brother."

I John 4:19-21

Let's be honest. Loving others can seem like an impossible thing to do. This is especially true about those we don't know or may have just met, or for those who have deeply offended us. This is why this principle is so important. It is only by the power of the Holy Spirit that we can love others like this. It's one thing to say intellectually that we love our enemy. But it is another thing altogether to have warm feelings in our hearts for those who want to harm us. If we have some measure of love like this in our hearts, then it is a sign that the Holy Spirit is working in us to transform us to be like Jesus.

How did Jesus love us? He sacrificed himself for us on the cross. What greater love is there than this?

Check yourself. Are you willing to become this kind of person?

A follower of Christ must love others that are underprivileged, needy, and living in poverty or despair. Such people in our society are often oppressed and exploited. Children specifically that are struggling to survive in this world do not get to experience their childhood innocence. They struggle to survive, which impacts their physical and emotional well-being.

Jesus has taught everyone to be compassionate and loving towards such community members and extend their hand by providing assistance to the needy. A Christian must extend a hand of compassion to every person that comes across as needy; love them in the name of Jesus. Doing this will help you develop an eternal relationship with God.

What if Your Love is Absent?

We must stop hating anyone and start loving everyone. Jesus' instructions were to judge nobody, but show mercy to all. They were to stop fighting and instead pray for their enemies. They were to quit hording and begin sharing their possessions. They were to avoid shoving petty religious rules down people's throats and start demonstrating humility, recognizing themselves to need grace.

If you think about it, the kingdom of heaven is a beautiful thing. It's a realm of peace and grace and abundance. We should all hope to see it take over.

And we do want God's kingdom, but inhabiting it while walking on the presently unredeemed earth, down here in the muck, is tough. Heaven's laws are contrary to everything our nature and culture tell us. Living the kingdom-of-heaven life is dangerous.

If you practice unconditional love, others absolutely will take advantage of you. They'll use up whatever you give them and come back demanding more and more until you're ruined. The violent among them will interpret your meekness as permission to rob, enslave, rape or murder you. The cynical will mock you.

If you obey heaven's rules, you're not stepping into a dreamy, mushy utopia. You're likely as not to get your throat cut by barbarians. Which is basically what happened to Jesus and his apostles.

Subsequent Christians have long tried to find a compromise, a way to nod at what Christ commanded without getting risky about it.

Instead of settling into even a Fifty-Fifty compromise between the heaven life and the earth life, we currently operate at about ten percent heaven and ninety percent earth. We give the Lord a tithe of our devotion. The devil gets the bulk. We'll do a couple of hours at a soup kitchen, so long as we can return home to our comfy recliners and not have to deal with any more messy people for another month.

It's not surprising, then, that the church generally and Christians individually have proved about as corrupt as the rest of our broken society.

What impact might we have if we actually began to quietly demonstrate God's unconditional, self-sacrificing love—full-time? Why, we might reform this world and its institutions without firing a shot or carrying a sign or sweeping a primary.

"But if anyone has the world's goods and sees his brother in need, yet closes his heart against him, how does God's love abide in him?"

1 John 3:17

We're not likely to find out. I don't claim I've managed to live out the laws of heaven, either. I'm just as intolerant and self-serving as the next guy.

Yet, occasionally, I'll catch a glimpse of Jesus' kingdom and what it teaches and what it calls me to be. I keep trying, incrementally, with more failures than successes, to enter it. [3]

Knowing this we must still focus on our duty and Jesus' command to love.

At the heart of Christianity is love – love for God, love for oneself, and love for others. It's the guiding principle that underpins every teaching, every scripture, and every action. A false Christian might wear the label but fails to embody this core principle. They might engage in divisive behavior, spread negativity, or fail to show kindness and understanding. If love is absent from their actions and their interactions with others, then no amount of religious talk or display can mask that. They are not living the true essence of Christianity.

Remember, an authentic Christian radiates love — in their words, their actions, and their approach to life. It's the ultimate sign of genuine faith.

Your most powerful testimony is how you treat people after the church service is over.

A True Christian has a Christian Heart

Having a Christian heart means putting our trust and faith in Jesus Christ, and committing to serve others and Him with the whole spirit in our hearts. When you follow Christ, you become a new person with a new mindset and thinking. Christians must have a heart that reflects the love, compassion, and mercy of Jesus Christ.

This means having a heart that is willing to forgive, that shows kindness and generosity to others, and that strives to live a life that is pleasing to God. It means putting others before ourselves and seeking to serve others, just as Christ did.

We must seek to honor God instead of going after worldly pursuits and selfish desires.

Once we commit to Christ, we learn to love God through the Holy Spirit. The Holy Spirit then works within us and molds us into righteous Christians. How we come to Christ isn't important, but come we must!

"My son, give me your heart and let your eyes delight in my ways,"
Proverbs 23:26

"For where your treasure is, there your heart will be also."

Matthew 6:21

Christians give only two and a half percent of their income to support their local churches. Only one percent of believers support Christian programs that they listen to regularly. 4

Jesus said;

"For where your treasure is, there your heart will be also."
Luke 12:34

Your credit card statements and checkbook ledgers will reveal where your true treasure is. Jesus gives us a statement about storing up security in our possessions;

"Do not lay up for yourselves treasures on earth, where moth and rust destroy and where thieves break in and steal, but lay up for yourselves treasures in heaven, where neither moth nor rust destroys and where thieves do not break in and steal. For where your treasure is, there your heart will be also. "The eye is the lamp of the body. So, if your eye is healthy, your whole body will be full of light, but if your eye is bad, your whole body will be full of darkness. If then the light in you is darkness, how great is the darkness! "No one can serve two masters, for either he will hate the one and love the other, or he will be devoted to the one and despise the other. You cannot serve God and money.
Matthew 6:19-24

Why is Having a Good Christian Heart Important?

It Reflects God's Character: As Christians, we are called to reflect the character of God, who is love. Having a good heart means showing love and compassion to others, just as God shows us.

It Impacts Others: Having a good heart can have a positive impact on those around us. Our kindness and love can inspire others to do the same, and can even draw non-believers closer to God.

Another reason why having a good Christian heart is important is because it allows us to reflect the love of Christ to the world around us. When we demonstrate love, kindness, and compassion to others, we show them the same love that Jesus demonstrated during his time on earth.

As Christians, we are called to be the hands and feet of Christ in the world, and having a good Christian heart is crucial to fulfilling that calling. By showing love and kindness to others, we can lead them to Christ and help them experience the same love that we have received.

Ultimately, having a good Christian heart is important because it allows us to glorify God and fulfill our purpose as his children. When we reflect the love of Christ to others, we bring glory to God and help build his kingdom on earth.

Having a good Christian heart means being motivated to make a positive impact on others and the world. It means actively seeking opportunities to help those in need and spread love and kindness wherever possible. By doing so, we can make a tangible difference in the lives of others and in the world around us.

Acts of kindness, generosity, and compassion can have a ripple effect, inspiring others to do the same and creating a chain reaction of positivity. This can have a profound impact not just on individuals, but on entire communities and societies.

Ultimately, living with a good Christian heart means using our time, talents, and resources to make the world a better place. As we work to serve others and spread love and compassion, we can help to create a more just, equitable, and peaceful world.

Having a good Christian heart is not only important for our relationships with others, but also for our relationship with God. When we strive to live according to His teachings, we deepen our faith and trust in Him, and experience a greater sense of peace and purpose.

As we grow in our faith and understanding, we are better able to connect with God through prayer, worship, and study of His word. By living a virtuous life and reflecting the love of Christ, we honor God and glorify Him in all that we do.

Ultimately, having a good Christian heart is about aligning ourselves with God's will and seeking to serve Him in all aspects of our lives. When we prioritize our relationship with God above all else, we can experience the true joy and fulfillment that comes from living a life of faith and obedience. Take the following steps each day:

1. **Make time for prayer:** Regular prayer is a crucial component of developing a good Christian heart. Find a time and place where you can be alone with God and commit to spending time in prayer each day.

2. **Meditate on Scripture:** Spend time each day reading and meditating on the Bible. This can help you gain a deeper understanding of God's word and how it applies to your life.

3. **Reflect on your actions:** Take time each day to reflect on your actions and motivations. Ask God to help you recognize areas where you need to improve and give you the strength to make positive changes.

4. **Practice gratitude:** Cultivate a spirit of gratitude by regularly thanking God for his blessings in your life. This can help you focus on the positive and develop a more positive outlook on life.

5. **Seek accountability:** Find a trusted Christian friend or mentor who can hold you accountable in your faith journey. Having someone to talk to and share your struggles with can be a great source of support and encouragement.

The Benefits of Prayer:

1. **Prayer Helps to Focus on God's Will:** Through prayer, we align our thoughts and desires with God's plan for us, making it easier to develop a heart that is in line with his.

2. **Prayer Encourages Reflection:** As we pray, we reflect on our actions, attitudes, and emotions. This reflection allows us to identify areas where we may need to change or improve in order to become more Christ-like.

3. **Prayer Provides Comfort and Strength:** Prayer can help us find peace and comfort during difficult times, and it can give us the strength to overcome challenges and temptations that may lead us astray from our Christian values.

4. **Prayer Encourages Gratitude:** Through prayer, we can express our gratitude for God's blessings in our lives. This fosters a heart of gratitude, which helps us to appreciate the goodness of others and to seek out opportunities to serve and give back.

5. **Prayer Connects Us to a Community:** Prayer is not just an individual act but can also connect us to a larger community of believers. This sense of community can help us develop a heart that is compassionate, empathetic, and caring towards others.

As real Christians we must practice forgiveness. We are called to forgive others as God has forgiven us. This can be a difficult task, but it's important to let go of anger and resentment towards those who have wronged us. Forgiveness allows us to move on and love others without judgement or bitterness.

Share your faith. Sharing the gospel message with others is a powerful way to show love and kindness. By sharing the hope and joy that comes from knowing Christ, we can bring light to someone's life and help them find meaning and purpose.

Be intentional with your words and actions. Every day presents opportunities to show love and kindness to others through our words and actions. It's important to be intentional with how we interact with those around us, striving to always show compassion, respect, and generosity.

Volunteering your time and talents to help others in need is a great way to show love and kindness. Whether it's serving at a homeless shelter, visiting a nursing home, or simply helping a neighbor with yard work, small acts of service can make a big impact.

Acts of service allow us to make a positive impact on the world and those around us. Through acts of service, we can show love and kindness to others and help improve their lives.

Jesus was the ultimate servant leader, and He taught us to love and serve others. When we engage in acts of service, we follow Jesus' example and show our commitment to living a Christian life.

Acts of service bring people together and help build stronger communities. When we work together to serve others, we create bonds of trust and friendship that can last a lifetime.

Serving others gives us a sense of purpose and meaning in our lives. It helps us focus on something beyond ourselves and can lead to greater satisfaction and fulfillment.

Through acts of service, we can strengthen our faith and deepen our relationship with God. When we serve others, we serve God, and we can feel his presence and love in our lives.

The Role of Forgiveness in Having an Authentic Christian Heart

Forgiveness is a central theme in the Christian faith. As Christians, we are called to forgive others, just as we have been forgiven by God. Forgiveness allows us to let go of resentment and anger, and frees us from the burden of holding onto grudges.

Forgiveness does not mean forgetting or excusing the wrong that was done, but rather it means choosing to release the offender from their debt to us. Forgiveness is an act of compassion and mercy, and it requires us to put aside our own feelings and to extend grace to others.

Forgiveness is not always easy, and it often requires us to confront our own pain and to work through our emotions. However, through prayer and reflection, we can find the strength to forgive others and to seek forgiveness ourselves.

Forgiveness is not a one-time event, but rather it is a process that requires ongoing effort and commitment. It is important to continually seek forgiveness and to extend forgiveness to others, as we are all fallible and in need of grace.

Forgiveness is not only beneficial for the individual, but it also has a positive impact on the broader community. When we forgive others, we model Christ's love and kindness, and we contribute to a culture of compassion and reconciliation.

Forgiveness can bring healing to both yourself and others, releasing negative emotions and enabling you to move forward in a positive way.

Forgiveness can restore relationships that have been damaged by hurt, anger, or betrayal, allowing for renewed trust and love.

Forgiveness frees us from the burden of carrying grudges and resentment, allowing us to live in peace and harmony with others.

Forgiveness provides an opportunity for personal growth and transformation, helping us to become more empathetic, compassionate, and loving individuals.

Forgiveness sets an example for others to follow, showing them the power of grace, mercy, and love in action. By forgiving those who have wronged us, we free ourselves from the burden of resentment and anger.

The Power of Gratitude

Gratitude is an important aspect of developing a positive attitude. It involves focusing on the good things in your life and expressing appreciation for them. By practicing gratitude regularly, you can increase your happiness and sense of well-being, as well as strengthen your relationships with others. Whether you keep a gratitude journal, say thank you more often, or simply take a few moments each day to reflect on the good in your life, practicing gratitude can have a profound impact on your outlook.

By focusing on the good in every situation and expressing appreciation for the blessings in your life, you can develop a mindset of abundance and joy that will help you navigate life's challenges with grace and resilience. [5]

"And He said to him, "'You shall love the Lord your God with all your heart, and with all your soul, and with all your mind.' This is the great and foremost commandment."

Matthew 22:37-38

Having Compassion

During a period of struggle in my life, I turned to a church friend who was vocal about his religious beliefs.

I was hoping for some comforting words, some empathy. Instead, he brushed off my struggles and quickly changed the subject to something trivial.

His lack of compassion was surprising, considering how he always preached about love and empathy in our community gatherings.

That's when it became clear to me. Being a Christian isn't just about attending church or quoting scripture.

It's about showing compassion, offering a shoulder to lean on during tough times. It's about empathizing with others and being there for them. This not only applies to our friends; it applies for all people, yes even the lost.

A false Christian might talk the talk, but when it comes to walking the walk, they falter.

What does the Bible say about Compassion?

The Hebrew and Greek words translated "compassion" in the Bible mean "to have mercy, to feel sympathy and to have pity." We know that, according to the Bible, God is "a compassionate and gracious God, slow to anger, abounding in love and faithfulness" (Psalm 86:15). Like all of God's attributes, His compassion is infinite and eternal. His compassions never fail; they are new every morning (Lamentations 3:22-23).

Jesus Christ, the Son of God, exemplified all of the Father's attributes, including His compassion. When Jesus saw His friends weeping at the grave of Lazarus, He felt compassion for them and wept alongside them (John 11:33-35). Moved with compassion for the suffering of others, Jesus healed the large crowds who came to Him

(Matthew 14:14), as well as individuals who sought His healing (Mark 1:40-41). When He saw the large crowds as sheep without a shepherd, His compassion led Him to teach them the things the false shepherds of Israel had abandoned. The priests and scribes were proud and corrupt; they despised the common people and neglected them, but Jesus had compassion on them, and He taught and loved them.

When asked what was the greatest commandment, Jesus responded that it is to love God with all our heart, mind and strength. But He added that the second commandment "is like it: 'Love your neighbor as yourself'" (Matthew 22:34-40). The Pharisee had asked Him which single command of God is the greatest, but Jesus provided two, stating not only what we are to do, but also how to do it. To love our neighbor as ourselves is the natural result of our loving devotion toward God.

The Bible is clear that compassion is an attribute of God and of God's people as well. [6]

God is compassionate. He is sympathetic to the suffering of His people. He sees our distress and takes pity on us. However, His compassion is more than mere sympathy and pity. God's compassion is related to His mercy, kindness, patience, grace, forgiveness, and love. In fact, some of these attributes are so related and intwined as to make clear separations between them difficult. God's compassion compels Him to take action.

God's sympathy for our lost and miserable state led Him not only to feel our pain, but to provide an atoning sacrifice for our guilt; this He did by sending His Son to die for our sins (Romans 5:8; Ephesians 2:1–10).

Jesus is the Father's most compassionate gift to humanity. It is only by and through faith in Jesus Christ that we are forgiven of our guilt and rescued from our deplorable condition (John 14:6; Acts 4:12).

Jesus is God in the flesh (John 1:14). He experienced human life and is able to sympathize with us fully (Hebrews 4:14–16). He lived a perfect life and modeled things like compassion for us. By observing the compassion of Christ, we catch glimpses of the compassion of the Father and see how we ourselves can show compassion to others (Philippians 2:1–11).

The compassion of Christ can be clearly seen in the Gospel narratives. For example, in Matthew 9:36, we observe Christ's compassion for the harassed and helpless. In Matthew 14:14, we see His compassion for those who are sick and suffer disease. In Matthew 15:32, we witness His compassion for those who hunger. In Luke 7:11–15, we hear of His compassion for the widowed who were especially vulnerable; therefore, He resurrected the widow's son and gave him back to her. In the case of Lazarus, Christ's compassion was so strong that He wept (John 11). When Jesus arrived graveside, He raised Lazarus from the dead and gave him back to his grieving relatives. No doubt Jesus Himself rejoiced greatly over the return of His friend.

The pinnacle of Christ's compassion can be observed at the cross of Calvary where He lay down His life for the sins of the world (John 3:16). Those who put their faith in Jesus are born again spiritually and receive the Holy Spirit. We are made new creations in Christ (2 Corinthians 5:17). This enables us to love God and our neighbors. We are commanded in Scripture to put on hearts of compassion as we relate to our fellow Christians (Colossians 3:12–15) and to those who have yet to hear the gospel and believe in Christ.

This compassion we are called to is not about emotions only, but is a call to action. True compassion encompasses both a gut level feeling of sympathy and pity as well as positive action taken on our part to relieve the suffering we observe (1 John 3:18). One of the most compassionate acts we can do is to share the good news of the gospel of Jesus Christ with those who do not know Him so that they might be restored to fellowship with Him. However, our compassion is not to be limited to the lost. We are commanded to have compassion on all people, but especially those who belong to the household of faith (Galatians 6:10) and more especially to those who are poor and powerless among us (James 1:27).

Jesus has given believers the Holy Spirit and commanded us to follow His promptings to be compassionate (Galatians 5:22–23). We must have Jesus' heart for the lost, hurt, wounded, poor, and needy souls of this world. Scripture makes it crystal clear that if we do not have compassion or love for each other, then we do not know God (1 John 3:17; 4:20). We cannot be void of compassion and still call ourselves Christians. Compassion is of paramount importance in revealing the genuineness of our faith in Christ. Compassion and love are how we are identified as Christ's disciples (John 13:34–35). Without it we are nothing but clanging cymbals (1 Corinthians 13:1–3). [7]

When Jesus was moved with compassion, He acted. He touched the leprous man and healed him. He laid hands on the blind men and opened their eyes to the world. He saw the hungry, weary crowds who thirsted for His words and hungered for His healing, and He fed them.

Praise God that the compassion of Jesus did more than just wish us well. Sympathy feels, but Jesus did. Healed. Fed. Taught. These are action verbs and they can teach us about the role of compassion in our lives.

What can we do in our daily lives to do compassion toward others? Here's where we get tripped up: compassion is often seen as an act of kindness toward a needy stranger, like giving a few dollars to the homeless veteran. Hit and run compassion is deeply important, but we're missing out if we're only looking for opportunities to help.

Compassion is administered daily. And most of the time, it's poured out on the people we interact with every day: Husbands, children, parents, the mom on the next park bench, the cashier at the convenience store, the police officer who just gave you a ticket for talking on your cell phone.

Whenever we practice compassion, we exercise our hearts and strengthen our spirits to be more like Jesus. Jesus's disciple, and witness to the Lord's compassion, Peter wrote:

Finally, all of you, have unity of mind, sympathy, brotherly love, a tender heart, and a humble mind. Do not repay evil for evil or reviling for reviling, but on the contrary, bless, for to this you were called, that you may obtain a blessing.

1 Peter 3:8-9

Our gracious God formed our hearts not only to love and serve others with compassion, but to be blessed by our obedience. When we bless others, we are blessed ourselves.

The steadfast love of the Lord never ceases; his mercies never come to an end; they are new every morning; great is your faithfulness.

Lamentations 3:22-23

Blessed are we to go, to do, and to give with compassion. 8

Our true priority should be seeking Christ and His kingdom above all else because if we do, we will have all that we need (Matt 6:33).

The Importance of Compassion and Empathy

Compassion and empathy are two crucial elements of having a good Christian heart. Compassion involves feeling concern and showing kindness towards others, especially those who are suffering. It requires a willingness to see the world from another's perspective and to act on their behalf. Empathy, on the other hand, is the ability to share in another's feelings, to feel what they feel, and to connect with them emotionally. Together, compassion and empathy help us to see and respond to the needs of others.

Loving the Lost!

"What man of you, having a hundred sheep, if he has lost one of them, does not leave the ninety-nine in the open country, and go after the one that is lost, until he finds it?

Luke 15:4

So let us be clear. Jesus did not come to help us get along, or teach us to take care of the poor, or to restore "social justice." To some, this assertion is a bold stroke, since they have been told just the opposite. This is because there are many noble people who are drawn to Jesus for His moral excellence (as they should be). However, often their admiration of His civic virtue has distracted them from a more important matter.

"Social justice" is not the Gospel. It was not Jesus' message. It was not why He came. His real message was much more radical. Jesus' teaching—and the Story itself—focuses on something else. Not on the works of *Christians*, but rather on the work of *Christ*.

Why did God come down? What was the reason He became a man? What did He come to earth to do?

Let's look at something in the Christmas story you may have not noticed. Consider the most important Christmas verse in the story that you will never see on a Christmas card, and you will never hear in a Christmas pageant because it is not in the accounts of Jesus' birth at all. In fact, it does not appear anywhere in the record of His life. Instead, you find it in a passage that speaks of blood and sacrifice and death. It is a section of the story recounting a ghastly system of slaughter where bulls and goats were bled out, their innocent lives forfeit on behalf of others who were the guilty ones.

The system of sacrifice served only as a temporary measure to cover man's moral wound for the moment. It would never do in the long run, and it was not meant to. No, man owes the debt, and in the long run man, not creatures, must pay. And only a sinless man—someone with no debt of his own—could cover the debt of another. And only a man who was more than a man could ever pay for the sins of multitudes.

And this brings us to the most important Christmas verse you will never hear on Christmas. Here it is:

Consequently, when Christ came into the world, He said;

"Sacrifices and offerings you have not desired, but a body have you prepared for me; in burnt offerings and sin offerings you have taken no pleasure. Then I said, 'Behold, I have come to do your will, O God, as it is written of me in the scroll of the book.'"

Hebrews 10:5-7

The story is saying that on that first Christmas, in some incredible way the eternal Son of God in a baby's body said to His Father, "Here I am. I will do as You have asked. I accept the body You have prepared for Me, the body that will bleed out in perfect payment for sin."

This is the answer to why Jesus came to earth. God's Son surrendered His sinless human self to be the future unblemished offering to save sinners perfectly and completely. 9

So, what does this have to do with saving the lost?

Jesus put it this way;

"For the Son of Man came to seek and to save the lost."

Luke 19:10

Jesus had just been criticized for going to the house of a "sinner." Jesus responded by affirming His mission was to save people who needed saving. Their reputation for sinfulness was not a reason to avoid them; rather, it was a reason to seek them out. Many times, during Christ's ministry, He sought to forgive those whom the self-righteous leaders of the day shunned. He sought out and saved the woman at the well and the Samaritans of her town (John 4:39–41), the sinful woman with the alabaster jar (Luke 7:37), and even one of His own disciples, Matthew, who had been a tax collector (Matthew 9:9).

In Matthew 9, once again Jesus was criticized for *"eating with tax collectors and sinners"* (verse 11), and once again Jesus responded by stating His mission: *"'I desire mercy, and not sacrifice.' For I came not to call the righteous, but sinners."* (verse 13). Jesus' goal was to save. It was a goal that He reached: *"I glorified you on earth, having accomplished the work that you gave me to do."* (John 17:4).

All through the Gospels, we see Jesus' call to repentance and forgive the worst of sinners. No one is too sinful to come to Him. In fact, He goes after those who are lost, as the parables of the lost sheep and lost coin show (Luke 15:1–10). In the story of the prodigal son, Jesus teaches that God will always welcome with open arms those who come to Him with a repentant heart (Luke 15:21–22; cf. Isaiah 57:15). Even today, Jesus continues to seek and save those who humbly place their faith in Him (Matthew 11:29; 18:3–4; Revelation 3:20). 10

So, if Jesus is out role model, then shouldn't we also have the same mission to save the lost? I think you know the answer!

God is glorified by the salvation of the lost. Nothing glorifies God more than the conversion of a sinner. As Christians, it is not enough to glorify God by living a righteous life, going to church, reading the Bible, and tithing regularly. Sure, those things please God, and indeed, He expects us to do them. But living right is not the only goal for those who are saved. To truly glorify God, you must work with all you're might for the salvation of the lost. As Christians, we are to follow in Jesus' steps. And Jesus said that his main purpose was to save sinners!

Therefore, we cannot truly follow Christ unless we also seek the salvation of the lost!

Being men and women in this present world, we must glorify God as Jesus did, by winning souls. Therefore, it is only natural for us, as Christians, to return the love that God had for us, by working with all our might to convert a sinner from the error of his way, and save a soul from death.

Every Christian should work with all his might for the salvation of the lost, because God has commanded us to do this work. The true believer does not need to read a verse in the Bible that expressly tells Christians to win souls. The Holy Spirit speaks to every saved person to have concern and deep consideration for the spiritual welfare of those people in the church, or in the world, that are not saved. Perhaps you have felt a deep desire to see someone converted to Christ before. That is God's calling to you. Listen to the voice of God, as He calls you to be interested in the salvation of the lost. Who knows, perhaps your influence on them may be used of God as a means of grace to draw them unto Christ.

As Christ, our main purpose in life is the business of winning souls for God. Like Him, each of us must strive to win souls. As Christ, we too have come to seek and to save the lost. We must follow this example, and be like Christ.

It is an awful thing to think of what it means to be lost. It is unpleasant to think of what it means to be lost now, to say nothing about what it means to be lost in Hell. What can we do to convert a person from sin and from its consequences? Our hearts are stirred when we hear of millions whose bodies are starved around the world, but what is this to millions whose souls are starving, who are in sin and far from God and without Christ? Isn't it better to save one perishing soul than to save ten million starving bodies?

Every authentic Christian has the love of God in them. This love is not meant for us to hold up inside, and keep to ourselves alone. Rather, Christian love motivates us to seek the conversion of sinners! As a matter of fact, uninhibited Christian love and concern for the lost should be the ultimate goal of every true believer. If we are to model ourselves after Jesus, and look to Him, not only as our physical, but also as our spiritual guide, it is most evident, that Jesus is ever burdened for sinners, and forever compassionate and loving toward them.

Our eternal reward depends upon our earnestness and sincere activity in soul winning. Every new soul won is a new jewel in our Savior's crown and a new jewel in our crown. If you want to be an authentic Christian, there is no better way to become one than by acting to save souls. Just as winning souls was the first work of Christ, so too, it should be the first work of every Christian. For a Christian to die and go to Heaven, without working to save lost souls, is like Christ returning to Heaven without having accomplished the task that God had sent Him forth to do on the Cross. It will be a shameful thing for us to live in glory, unable to really enjoy the presence of the Lord since you were not one of His good and faithful servants.

Working to win souls will give you a crown in the Kingdom. And every soul that is won to Christ, that is directly attributable to your ministry, will add a jewel to your crown, as well.

We must seek the salvation of the lost by prayer. Praying for the lost is not our only duty, but it is our first duty. We accomplish more in that way than in any other single way. We are praying to God to save them. The earnest prayer for a soul to be saved is heard by God. Thus, praying for the lost to be awakened and converted is the most important prayer we can do for them.

It is even better to pray specifically for each lost soul, by name, and with much reflection and thought about the person. Develop a deep desire to see them saved. How do we do this? By praying for them every day, or whenever the person you are praying for crosses your mind. When you come into this person's company and talk to them, the Holy Spirit may reveal to them that you have been praying for them, and truly do love them, as Jesus does. God can use you in this way to open sinners up, by making them see the love of God in you.

Prayer is the first thing but not the only thing. Begin trying to lead others to Christ. How do we lead others to Christ? Bring them to church to hear the Gospel! Sermons can point a lost soul in the direction of Christ. By bringing a lost person to church to hear sound gospel preaching, you are leading them to Jesus. You are glorifying God and actually doing something to fill his house, not just passively praying in a dry or meaningless way, for the lost to come in and be saved. We may seldom see a lost soul wander into the church looking for salvation. We must take action and invite them in. People have to be brought in to church. Christ said, *"Go out to the highways and hedges and compel people to come in, that my house may be filled"* (Luke 14:23). This is how we lead the lost to Christ.

As Christians, we should be in training all the time for the work of winning souls. Everywhere we go, anything that we are doing, we must strive to always be training. Invite the lost to church no matter where you are at, or what you are doing. Ask for God's help and blessing as you do it. Train yourself! It's good for you!

"Let him know that whoever brings back a sinner from his wandering will save his soul from death and will cover a multitude of sins."

James 5:20

Seek and obtain God's power. Every Christian man and woman can have the power of the Holy Spirit. Give yourself wholly to God. Ask for

TWO KINDS OF CHRISTIANS

His power. Believe that He will give it to you. Claim it by faith and go to work for Christ! 11

The Apostle Paul famously said that his "heart's desire" and his "prayer to God" is that his fellow Jews "may be saved" (Romans 10:1). The problem was that these "kinsmen according to the flesh" were lost—bound for an eternity without God—which filled Paul's heart with "great sorrow and unceasing anguish" (Romans. 9:2-3).

We must keep in our mind the terrible reality of entering eternity without Christ.

Whoever believes in the Son has eternal life; whoever does not obey the Son shall not see life, but the wrath of God remains on him.
John 3:36

"The saying is trustworthy and deserving of full acceptance, that Christ Jesus came into the world to save sinners, of whom I am the foremost. But I received mercy for this reason, that in me, as the foremost, Jesus Christ might display his perfect patience as an example to those who were to believe in him for eternal life."
1 Timothy 1:15-16

We must think of Our Joy at the Conversion of One Lost Soul.

"For what is our hope or joy or crown of boasting before our Lord Jesus at his coming? Is it not you?"
1 Thessalonians 2:19

We must think of God's Amazing Grace to Us in Christ. We must Pray for God to Increase Our Love for the Lost

"And may the Lord make you increase and abound in love for one another and for all, as we do for you,"
1 Thessalonians 3:12

God has a strong desire that men and women be saved and that none would die without Christ. If you have no desire or interest to share the gospel with the lost, then you do not have the same kind of desire that God has for those who will perish without Christ. What breaks the heart of God should break the heart of those who He has redeemed. It's as if we had a cure for cancer and we refuse to share this cure with those who are dying. We fear being rejected, scorned, or embarrassed and so we do not witness to people about Jesus Christ. We fear men more than God. Peter, Isaiah, Ezekiel, and Paul all understood this. Paul told Timothy that God;

"Wants all men to be saved and to come to a knowledge of the truth."

1 Timothy 2:4

God has said; *"For I take no pleasure in the death of anyone, declares the Sovereign LORD. Repent and live!"*

Ezekiel 18:32

Real Christians want others to love the Lord. Consider what Jesus said in the Great Commission.

"Go therefore and make disciples of all nations...teaching them to observe all that I have commanded you."

Matthew 28:19-20

This principle is built into the Christian experience. It is the primary command in scripture that tells us what we should be doing with our Christian life. If you have no desire for others to know Jesus or to grow to maturity in Christ, then you may not have your heart right with the Lord.

To be able to seek out the lost and to share the gospel with the lost, you must go out into the world. Yes, we must fellowship with other believers, but there must also be a time to go to the lost. This doesn't mean hanging out in bars or going to strip clubs, but there are plenty of places to go where the lost also go. Restaurants, grocery stores, shopping malls, outdoor parks, and yes...even at church.

"But in your hearts honor Christ the Lord as holy, always being prepared to make a defense to anyone who asks you for a reason for the hope that is in you; yet do it with gentleness and respect."

1 Peter 3:15

We must go all out to save lost souls. If we are to imitate God in the task of missions and evangelism, we must show at least some effort in finding the lost as we do in looking for lost pets or valuables. After all, aside from His glory, human beings are more important to our Creator than anything else. He has a passion to seek and to save the lost, for that is why Christ became incarnate (Luke 19:1–10). Moreover, Luke 15 shows us that there is great joy in heaven when one sinner repents. The Lord throws a "party," as it were, whenever lost people are found and whenever they believe on the Lord Jesus Christ.

We, too, were once lost in sin before the Lord found us (Ephesians 2:11–12). And Christ found and saved us through the ministry of others, whether through our family, a friend, or someone else. Let us be used to seek and save the lost.

God cares about the souls of every one of His image bearers and so must we. Our friends, family, coworkers, neighbors, and acquaintances who do not know Christ will endure God's wrath forever if they do not trust Jesus before they die. When God sends lost people our way, we must be ready to share our testimony and the gospel with them. Let us look for the lost among all people so we can make a difference in the world. 12

What kind of Christian are you. The Christian that loves and cares for the lost, or the Christian who doesn't?

GLORIFYING GOD

"For many, of whom I have often told you and now tell you even with tears, walk as enemies of the cross of Christ. Their end is destruction, their god is their belly, and they glory in their shame, with minds set on earthly things."

Philippians 3:18-19

Definition: "Glorifying" means feeling and thinking and acting in ways that reflect God's greatness, that make much of God, that give evidence of the supreme greatness of all His attributes and the all-satisfying beauty of his manifold perfections.

The question is; are we glorifying God or ourself? How do we know the answer?

Here are five clues we can use to test who we are glorifying:

1. **Displaying in public what should be kept in private.**
   The Pharisees are a primary example. Because they saw their lives as glorious, they were quick to parade that glory before watching eyes. The more you think you've arrived and the less you see yourself as daily needing rescuing grace, the more you will tend to be self-referencing and self-congratulating. You work to get greater glory even when you aren't aware that you're doing it. You tend to tell personal stories that make you the hero. You will find ways, in public settings, of talking about private acts of faith.

Because you think you're worthy of acclaim, you will seek the acclaim of others by finding ways to present yourself as "godly."

2. Being too self-referencing.

We all know it, we've all seen it, we've all been uncomfortable with it, and we've all done it. Proud people tend to talk about themselves a lot. Proud people tend to like their opinions more than the opinions of others. Proud people think they know and understand more than others. Proud people think they've earned the right to be heard. Proud people, because they are basically proud of what they know and what they've done, talk a lot about both. Proud people don't reference weakness. Proud people don't talk about failure. Proud people don't confess sin. So proud people are better at putting the spotlight on themselves than they are at shining the light of their stories and opinions on God's glorious and utterly undeserved grace.

3. Talk when we should listen.

When you think you've arrived, you are quite proud of and confident in your opinions. You trust your opinions, so you are not as interested in the opinions of others as you should be. You will tend to want your thoughts, perspectives, and viewpoints to win the day in any given meeting or conversation. This means you will be way more comfortable than you should be with dominating a gathering with your talk. You will fail to see that in a multitude of counsel there is wisdom. You will fail to see the essential ministry of the body of Christ in your life. You will fail to recognize your bias and spiritual blindness. So, you won't come to meetings formal or informal with a personal sense of need for what others have to offer, and you will control the talk more than you should.

4. Being quiet when we should speak.

Self-glory can go the other way as well. People who are too self-confident, who unwittingly attribute to themselves what could only have been accomplished by grace, often see meetings as a waste of time. Because they are proud, they are too independent, so meetings tend to be viewed as an irritating and unhelpful interruption of an already overburdened schedule. And when their ideas are on the table and being debated, they don't jump into the fray, because they think that their opinion doesn't need to be defended. Self-glory will cause you to speak too much when you should listen and to feel no need to speak when you should.

5. **Caring too much about what people think about us.**

When you have fallen into thinking that you're something, you want people to recognize the something. Again, you see this in the Pharisees: personal assessments of self-glory always lead to glory-seeking behavior. People who think they have arrived can become all too aware of how others respond to them. Because you're hyper-vigilant, watching the way the people in your ministry respond, you probably don't even realize how you do things for self-acclaim.

If you are a Christian, you understand that glorifying God is the ultimate, absolute, all-pervasive reason for being and doing everything we do.

God is seeking to be glorified in us. God will not share His glory with another. And why should He? He is God! He deserves all glory, honor and praise.

"I am the LORD; that is my name! I will not yield my glory to another or my praise to idols."

Isaiah 42:8

Our chief purpose as Christians is to glorify God and to enjoy Him forever. Too often we may be guilty of making ourselves look good and rob God of His glory. David did this once when he ordered a census of his troops. This was prideful and arrogant of David because his real strength was in God and not in his own might. This is why God punished David. When we seek to glorify ourselves or our own accomplishments, it's as if we are robbing God of what is rightfully His. When we take credit for things, we strip God of some of His glory.

"But he gives more grace. Therefore, it says, "God opposes the proud but gives grace to the humble."

James 4:6

How do we glorify God?

"Or do you not know that your body is a temple of the Holy Spirit within you, whom you have from God? You are not your own, for you were bought with a price. So, glorify God in your body."

1 Corinthians 6:19-20

Our actions should reflect Christ in us and when others see Jesus living in us, others are attracted to Christ. And when we boast about anything, let it be that we are who and what we are, all because of Christ Who lives in us.

"A man can no more diminish God's glory by refusing to worship Him than a lunatic can put out the sun by scribbling the word, 'darkness' on the walls of his cell" – C. S. Lewis

To glorify God is to honor Him with praise or worship. God is glorious; that is, He is great and magnificent—He is exceptionally grand in His nature and deeds.

"Full of splendor and majesty is his work."

Psalm 111:3

When we glorify God, we acknowledge His greatness and splendor and laud Him for it. When we "give Him glory," as all the world is told to do in Revelation 14:7, we direct our praise, adoration, thanksgiving, and worship to Him who alone is worthy.

Scripture makes our responsibility to glorify God evident from cover to cover. First Chronicles 16:8–36 presents a model for giving glory to God. As Asaph is installed as the chief minister before the ark of God, David instructs him in the method of worship:

- Give thanks to the Lord (verse 8)
- Proclaim the greatness of God's name (verse 8)
- Tell the whole world what God has done (verses 8–9, 24)
- Sing to the Lord (verses 9, 23)
- Glory, or exult, in His name (verse 10)
- Rejoice in Him (verse 10)
- Seek out the Lord and trust in His power (verse 11)
- Remember all the Lord's mighty deeds (verse 12)
- Ascribe glory to Him because it is His due (verses 28–29).
- Bring an offering to God (verse 29).
- Worship the Lord (verse 29)
- Give thanks to God for His goodness and love (verse 34)
- Cry out to God for deliverance (verse 35)

In Asaph's time, the offerings were in accordance with the Law of Moses; today, we are to offer our bodies as a living sacrifice,

I appeal to you therefore, brothers, by the mercies of God, to present your bodies as a living sacrifice, holy and acceptable to God, which is your spiritual worship.

Romans 12:1

El Elyon, the 'Most High' God, is the possessor of all true majesty and resplendence. Glory is His by virtue of His nature, and He rightfully refuses to share it with others:

"I am the Lord; that is my name! I will not yield my glory to another or my praise to idols."

Isaiah 42:8

By virtue of who God is, we have an obligation to glorify God at all times (1 Corinthians 10:31). Those who refuse to glorify God face severe judgment, as witnessed by the example of Herod seizing God's glory in Acts 12:21–23.

We can, of course, glorify God with our words of praise and thanksgiving. We can also glorify God through our works of service for Him. Jesus said, "Let your light shine before others, that they may see your good deeds and glorify your Father in heaven" (Matthew 5:16). Bearing fruit for the kingdom of God also brings glory to Him (John 15:8). Even in our manner of death, we can glorify God (see John 21:19).

To glorify God is to extol His attributes, praise His works, trust His name, and obey His Word. He is holy, faithful, merciful, gracious, loving, majestic, sovereign, powerful, and omniscient—and that's just for starters. His works are wonderful, wise, marvelous, and fearfully complex. His Word is "perfect . . . trustworthy . . . right . . . radiant . . . pure . . . firm . . . precious" (Psalm 19:7–10). His salvation is astonishing, timely, and near. No matter how loudly or widely we proclaim the glory of God, He is worthy of more.

"O come to the Father through Jesus the Son, and give Him the glory, great things He has done!" "To God Be the Glory," Fanny Crosby. 1

In Exodus God reveals himself as God, as personal, as glorious, and as passionate to be known for the glorious personal God that He is.

"I Am Who I Am"

In Exodus 3:12–15. God has come to Moses and told him to go down to Egypt and tell the Israelites God is going to deliver them from bondage.

He said, "But I will be with you, and this shall be the sign for you, that I have sent you: when you have brought the people out of Egypt, you shall serve God on this mountain." Then Moses said to God, "If I come to the people of Israel and say to them, 'The God of your fathers has sent me to you,' and they ask me, 'What is his name?' what shall I say to them?" God said to Moses, "I am who I am." And he said, "Say this to the people of Israel: 'I am has sent me to you.'" God also said to Moses, "Say this to the people of Israel: 'The Lord, the God of your fathers, the God of Abraham, the God of Isaac, and the God of Jacob, has sent me to you.' This is my name forever, and thus I am to be remembered throughout all generations."

They ask me my name, God says, and I will tell you three things in response to their request. First (verse 14), "God said to Moses, 'I Am Who I Am.'" He did not say that was his name. He wanted first for Moses to be in awe of who He is: "I Am Who I Am." And it seems that God would say this to us right now. You want to ask about what it means to glorify me, to do everything to my glory? Let me tell you something first. Let it sink in that I AM. Before you talk about me or do anything for me, be amazed that I exist. I absolutely am. This is first. This is foundational. This is of infinite importance.

Second (verse 14), "God said to Moses, "I am who I am." And He said, "Say this to the people of Israel: 'I am has sent me to you.'" He still hasn't given Moses his name. He is building a bridge between his being and his name, which we will see in verse 15. Here He simply puts the statement of his being in the place of his name. Say, "I Am has sent me to you." The one who is — who absolutely is — sent me to you. This is not yet his name. It's the basis of his name.

Third (verse 15), "God also said to Moses, "Say this to the people of Israel: 'The Lord, the God of your fathers, the God of Abraham, the God of Isaac, and the God of Jacob, has sent me to you.' This is my name forever, and thus I am to be remembered throughout all generations. "This is my name forever," referring to Yahweh (LORD).

Finally, He gives us his name. It's almost always translated LORD (all caps) in the English Bible. But the Hebrew would be pronounced something like, "Yahweh," and is built on, or associated with, the word for "I Am." So, every time we hear the word Yahweh (or the short form Yah, which you hear every time you sing "hallelu-jah," "praise Yahweh"), or every time you see LORD in the English Bible, you should think: this is a proper name (like Peter or James or John) built out of the word for "I Am" and reminding us each time that God absolutely is.

What Does It Mean That God Is?

What does it mean that God gives himself a personal name essentially meaning "I am who I am?" What does it mean to be Yahweh? What does it mean for God to be? Why does God make it His purpose that Israel and all the nations know Him by this name?

Here are a few answers for starters — The foundation of all His Glory:

1. **That "God is" means He never had a beginning.** This staggers the mind. Every child asks, "Who made God?" And every wise parent says, "Nobody made God. God simply is. And always was. No beginning."

2. **That "God is" means God will never end.** If He did not come into being; He cannot go out of being, because He is being. He is what is. There is no place to go outside of being. There is only He. Before He creates, that's all that is: God.

3. **That "God is" means God is absolute reality.** There is no reality before Him. There is no reality outside of Him unless He wills it and makes it. He is not one of many realities before He creates. He is simply there as absolute reality. He is all that was eternally. No space, no universe, no emptiness. Only God. Absolutely there. Absolutely all.

4. **That "God is" means that God is utterly independent.** He depends on nothing to bring Him into being or support Him or counsel Him or make Him what He is. That is what the word "absolute" being means. It's what the linguistic construction "I am who I am" means.

5. **That "God is" means rather that everything that is not God depends totally on God.** All that is not God is secondary, and dependent. The entire universe is utterly secondary. Not primary. It came into being by God and stays in being moment by moment on God's decision to keep it in being.

6. **That "God Is" means all the universe is by comparison to God as nothing.** Contingent, dependent reality is to absolute, independent reality as a shadow to substance. As an echo to a thunderclap. As a bubble to the ocean. All that we see, all that we are amazed by in the world and in the galaxies, is, compared to God, as nothing. "All the nations are as nothing before Him, they are accounted by Him as less than nothing and emptiness" (Isaiah 40:17).

7. **That "God is" means that God is constant.** He is the same yesterday, today, and forever. He cannot be improved. He is not becoming anything. He is who He is. There is no development in God. No progress. Absolute perfection cannot be improved.

8. **That "God is" means that He is the absolute standard of truth and goodness and beauty.** There is no law-book to which He looks to know what is right. No almanac to establish facts. No guild to determine what is excellent or beautiful. He himself is the standard of what is right, what is true, what is beautiful.

9. **That "God is" means God does whatever He pleases and it is always right and always beautiful and always in accord with truth.** There are no constraints on Him from outside Him that

could hinder Him in doing anything He pleases. All reality that is outside of Him He created and designed and governs as the absolute reality. So, He is utterly free from any constraints that don't originate from the counsel of his own will.

10. **That "God is" means that He is the most important and most valuable reality and the most important and most valuable person in the universe.** He is more worthy of interest and attention and admiration and enjoyment than all other realities, including the entire universe.

"God is". That's the first thing He reveals. This is the God we are to glorify.

Yahweh is not a generic term. The fact that it is translated LORD could be misleading, since Lord is a title not a name like Mary. But Yahweh is a personal name. In Exodus 3:15, God said to Moses, "Say this to the people of Israel, 'Yahweh, the God of your fathers, the God of Abraham, the God of Isaac, and the God of Jacob, has sent me to you.' This [Yahweh] is my name forever, and thus I am to be remembered throughout all generations."

God was not content to be known only by divine attributes. He means to be known by name. That's why He gave himself a name and then made it his identity so many times in the Bible.

One reason He put such an emphasis on the revelation of his name is that persons relate personally by name. If you only call someone by a title, you probably don't have a personal relationship. God means to be called upon by name. Yahweh is not a title. Every time you see all caps LORD in the Bible, think: I am calling God by his personal name.

Yahweh Is Glorious

Now we turn to the third thing God revealed about himself. First that He is. Second that He is personal. Third that He is glorious.

You can see the connection between God's glory and his name most clearly in Exodus 14. In verse 2, God says to Moses, "Tell the people of Israel to turn back and encamp in front of Pi-hahiroth." Now this seemed crazy. It was backward. They were almost free. Why go backward? God's answer: Because it will trick Pharaoh into thinking they are lost in the wilderness. He will be hardened against them and against God and will go out to capture them. And God will get one more opportunity to show the glory of his name in utterly defeating the arrogant Egyptians in the Red Sea. Verses 3–4 (this is Yahweh talking):

For Pharaoh will say of the people of Israel, "They are wandering in the land; the wilderness has shut them in." And I will harden Pharaoh's heart, and He will pursue them, and I will get glory over Pharaoh and all his host, and the Egyptians shall know that I am Yahweh.

And so, it happens. Pharaoh pursues the Israelites and traps them at the Red Sea. Then God says:

"Lift up your staff, and stretch out your hand over the sea and divide it, that the people of Israel may go through the sea on dry ground. And I will harden the hearts of the Egyptians so that they shall go in after them, and I will get glory over Pharaoh and all his host, his chariots, and his horsemen. And the Egyptians shall know that I am Yahweh, when I have gotten glory over Pharaoh, his chariots, and his horsemen."

Exodus 14:16–18

So, verse 4: *"I will get glory over Pharaoh and all his host, and the Egyptians shall know that I am Yahweh."* Verse 17: *"I will get glory over Pharaoh and all his host."* Verse 18: *"The Egyptians shall know that I am Yahweh, when I have gotten glory over Pharaoh, his chariots, and his horsemen."*

They will know I am Yahweh when I reveal My glory. But this can't mean merely that they will know that God's name is Yahweh. Doing these miracles doesn't put a name in their ear. What they know, when they see his glory, is something about what it means to be called Yahweh, the God who is. It means He has great glory. Greater glory than the greatest empires of the world. To be Yahweh is to be supremely glorious — great, awesome, beautiful.

God reveals himself as the God who is. Second, He reveals himself as personal. Third He reveals himself as supremely glorious. And finally, He reveals that He is passionate to be known for the glorious, personal God that He is.

This truth comes to us with massive implications for how we live our lives and do our ministry. God is passionately committed to making himself known as glorious above all other glories in the universe — all other competing glories in your life and on your campus.

If it has been clear that God is who He is, and if it has been clear that God reveals himself with a personal name, not just a title, and if it is clear that this God is glorious, it is crystal clear that God is passionate to be known as the glorious personal Yahweh that He is. The dominance of this point in the story of the Exodus is unmistakable.

"You shall know that I am Yahweh your God, who has brought you out from under the burdens of the Egyptians."

Exodus 6:7

"The Egyptians shall know that I am Yahweh, when I stretch out my hand against Egypt and bring out the people of Israel from among them."

Exodus 7:5

"By this you shall know that I am Yahweh. . .. I will strike the water that is in the Nile, and it shall turn into blood."

Exodus 7:17

"That you may know that there is no one like Yahweh our God."

Exodus 8:10

"No swarms of flies shall be in Goshen, that you may know that I am Yahweh in the midst of the earth."

Exodus 8:22

"For this purpose, I have raised you up, Pharaoh, to show you my power, so that my name may be proclaimed in all the earth."

Exodus 9:16

God has revealed himself to us as a God who is passionate to make known the glory of his name — not the pronunciation of it, as if this were magic, but the reality of it — the God who absolutely is, the God who is personal and the God who is supremely glorious.

And He has never ceased to be this God with this passion. This God of the Exodus is worshipped and celebrated in the Psalms.

"Our fathers, when they were in Egypt, did not consider your wondrous works; they did not remember the abundance of your steadfast love, but rebelled by the sea, at the Red Sea. Yet he saved them for his name's sake, that he might make known his mighty power."

Psalm 106:7–8

This God of the Exodus is worshipped and celebrated in the prophets.

"Then he remembered the days of old, of Moses and his people. Where is he who brought them up out of the sea with the shepherds of his flock? Where is he who put in the midst of them his Holy Spirit,

who caused his glorious arm to go at the right hand of Moses, who divided the waters before them to make for himself an everlasting name."

Isaiah 63:11–12

"But I am the Lord your God from the land of Egypt; you know no God but me, and besides me there is no savior."

Hosea 13:4

And the God of the Exodus has come into history in the person of Jesus Christ our Lord. That's why the baby fled to Egypt — so that Hosea's prophecy would be fulfilled

"And he rose and took the child and his mother by night and departed to Egypt and remained there until the death of Herod. This was to fulfill what the Lord had spoken by the prophet, "Out of Egypt I called my son."

Matthew 2:14-15

So, this Jesus fulfills the destiny of his people as the new Israel, and the new Passover (1 Corinthians 5:7), and the new Deliverer who would make a new Exodus for his people out of the bondage of sin, just as we see on the mount of transfiguration.

"And behold, two men were talking with him, Moses and Elijah, who appeared in glory and spoke of his departure, which he was about to accomplish at Jerusalem."

Luke 9:30–31

And when He came to that night in Jerusalem, Jesus was in great distress, and He cried out to God.

"Now is my soul troubled. And what shall I say? 'Father, save me from this hour'? But for this purpose, I have come to this hour. Father, glorify your name." Then a voice came from heaven: "I have glorified it, and I will glorify it again."

John 12:27–28:

And every one of us who has been delivered from bondage through what happened on the cross the next morning, know that we owe our life to the passion of Jesus for the glory of the name of God. Which is why 1 John 2:12 says, *"Your sins are forgiven for his name's sake."*

The Personal Name Jesus

And if, by the way, you wonder how the personal name Yahweh relates to the personal name, Jesus, consider these two amazing things. Jesus is from the Greek form of Joshua, which is built on the personal name of God ("Ja") and the Hebrew word for "salvation." So, Joshua and Jesus mean, "Yahweh saves," or, "Yahweh is salvation." An angel told Joseph, "You shall call his name Jesus, for He will save his people from their sins" (Matthew 1:21). Who will save his people? Yahweh will. That's what the name means.

It even gets more amazing when we hear Paul say of the risen Jesus in Philippians 2:11, *"Every tongue will confess that Jesus Christ is LORD, to the glory of God the Father."* That is a quote from Isaiah 45:23 where Yahweh is the one to whom every knee shall bow and every tongue confess. Paul is saying that in the end, we will see that Jesus is, in fact, Yahweh incarnate. You don't have to choose between knowing Him personally as Yahweh and knowing Him personally as Jesus. In fact, you dare not choose.

God the Father and God the Son brought God's people out of the Egypt of sin and slavery into the freedom and everlasting glory of sonship for the very same reason that God brought Israel out of Egypt in the Old Testament. That He might get glory over sin and Satan and Hell and all the principalities and powers that brought Jesus to the cross and all the world systems that rise up against his people—that He might get glory over them and all the world might know that Jesus, the crucified and risen one, is Yahweh, the glorious personal God who is.

This is what God is calling you into. The reason you should glorify God in everything is that God glorifies God in everything — that Jesus glorified God in everything. 2

So, whether you eat or drink, or whatever you do, do all to the glory of God.

1 Corinthians 10:31

What kind of Christian are you? The Christian that glorifies yourself, or the Christian that glorifies God?

BECOMING LIKE JESUS

For I have given you an example, that you also should do just as I have done to you."

John 13:15

John makes this point clear for us, too: we do what Jesus did. Jesus served his disciples and tells us, therefore, that we should serve one another. Jesus says that his humility is an example for us — that we do what He does. And this means, profoundly, that one of the ways we identify with our Savior is by caring for others in the same manner He has cared for us. We show ourselves to be his disciple when we humble ourselves and seek the good of others at our own expense.

This is important because there is a degree of suffering, we will experience in serving one another. It always costs *something* to seek someone else's good, and there will be times when it feels like we're not getting any encouraging return on our investments. In these moments, because of Jesus's example, we know it doesn't mean we turn and run, but instead press in and hold on. When the serving gets especially tough, we shouldn't necessarily serve less, but perhaps more. And in doing that, we go deeper with Jesus.

"You didn't have to reach a certain status of friendship for Jesus to serve you." [1]

A Real Christian Becomes like Jesus Christ

Those who put faith in the work of Jesus Christ must trust and replicate it in behavior. The behavior of a real Christian reflects, mirrors, and resembles Christ and his characteristics. You should be merciful and gracious to others. Behaving like Christ also refers to loving, forgiving, and praying for the enemies; striving for justice; and caring for vulnerable, abused, poor, orphaned, widowed, underprivileged, needy, and sick. Moreover, being like Jesus means serving and welcoming the marginalized groups and individuals of society.

However, what makes someone a Christian is not limited to doing good work and pleasant outward behavior, as the condition of our heart while performing the deeds matters the most. Being a follower and supporter of Jesus extends beyond our acts, but the intention with which they are performed is crucial.

"And calling the crowd to him with his disciples, he said to them, "If anyone would come after me, let him deny himself and take up his cross and follow me."

Mark 8:34

To become more like Jesus, we all need:

1. Unconditional Love

"Greater love has no one than this, than to lay down one's life for his friends."

John 15:13

The King of the Universe, The Creator of all things, gave up His throne, His beauty, His glory, and His position to come and die for you and me.

Are you loving unconditionally? Do you love the beggar the same way that you love the pastor in your church?

Every single born-again believer can love the way that God has asked us to. The Word of God says that The Love of God has been shed in our hearts by the Holy Spirit. So, God's love is already inside of you; you just have to bring it out.

Love like Jesus did; love the sinner. Your love is a testimony of God's love for them.

2. Prayerful Life

"But Jesus often withdrew to lonely places and prayed".

Luke 5:16

Jesus often withdrew to lonely places and prayed. Jesus spent time daily with The Father in prayer. Jesus knew how important it was to be connected and have a personal relationship with The Father. You can only have a personal relationship with someone you spend time with. Is spending time in prayer with The Lord a priority in your life?

3. Forgiveness

Jesus said;

"Father, forgive them, for they do not know what they are doing."

Luke 23:24

They put a crown of thorns on His head. They nailed Him to the cross and were casting lots on his clothes. Jesus could've opened His mouth and called a thousand angels. In His mouth He had the power to end it all. But He only opened his mouth to ask for forgiveness for those who were crucifying Him. It is not easy to forgive someone who has hurt you or a loved one deeply. It's not easy, but with God's help, we can do it. We must do it. The Bible tells us that we must forgive if we want to be forgiven. So, forgiveness is not a suggestion; forgiveness is a command.

4. Humility

"For even the Son of Man did not come to be served, but to serve, and to give his life as a ransom for many."

Mark 10:45

Even though Jesus was the King of Kings, He didn't come to be served as a King. He came to serve. A lot of people get humility wrong. Being humble doesn't mean that you are a wimp or that you put yourself down and let people walk all over you. Being humble is surrendering yourself under the mighty hand of God. Knowing that you are His child and that you are here on Earth to love and to serve others. Being humble is putting God and His will first. To treat and to love others as you would like them to treat you, and be a servant.

5. Study the Word of God

"When they did not find him, they went back to Jerusalem to look for him. After three days they found him in the temple courts, sitting among the teachers, listening to them and asking them questions."

Luke 2:45-46

Jesus was just a boy in this story and was "lost" for three days. Where was He? He was at church, listening and studying The Word of God. This story is not written just to add extra adventures to the life of Jesus. This story is written to show us how important it is for us to study the Bible. When Jesus was tempted by the devil, every single one of his responses was The Word of God. He used it as a sword against the devil, and He won. In the same way, we need to study the Bible so we can be spiritually strong and learn how to use the best weapon we have against the devil.

6. Compassion

"But when He saw the multitudes, He was moved with compassion for them, because they were weary and scattered, like sheep having no shepherd."

Matthew 9:36

Jesus was moved with compassion for the people that He came to save. Compassion means sympathetic pity and concern for the sufferings or misfortunes of others. In the world we live right now, people only worry about themselves and "what is in it for me?" We have become so self-absorbed that we have forgotten to have compassion for other people. Compassion is not something that you practice during Christmas time. We must be compassionate 365 days per year; it should be part of who we are. Being compassionate makes you more like Christ.

7. Seek First the Kingdom of God

"But seek first his kingdom and his righteousness, and all these things will be given to you as well."

Matthew 6:33

Jesus devoted His life to the work of the ministry, to do His Father's will, which was to bring the kingdom of God to this earth. Are you making the Kingdom of God a priority in your life? In your house? With your family? What are you doing to fulfill the great commission that Jesus told us to do? After all, fulfilling the great commission is God's will for your life.

"Go therefore and make disciples of all nations, baptizing them in[a] the name of the Father and of the Son and of the Holy Spirit."

Mathew 28:19

8. Self-Control

"He was led like a sheep to the slaughter, and as a lamb before its shearer is silent, so he did not open his mouth."

Acts 8:32

Even in the most difficult moment of His life, Jesus exercised self-control. With just one word, all His suffering could've ended, but He had self-control and stayed focused on doing the job that He came here to do. The Christian life is difficult, whether we like it or not we will encounter hardships. Self-control is what's going to keep you holding on to your faith and trusting God. Self-control will

TWO KINDS OF CHRISTIANS

keep you from falling into sin. Self-control will keep you from being run over by your feelings and your circumstances. Self-control will keep you rooted and grounded on the Word of God.

9. Authority

"Just then a man in their synagogue who was possessed by an impure spirit cried out, "What do you want with us, Jesus of Nazareth? Have you come to destroy us? I know who you are–the Holy One of God!" And Jesus rebuked him, saying, "Be quiet, and come out of him!"

Mark 1:23

Jesus knew who He was and the authority He had. He rebuked demons, He spoke and calmed the storms, He ordered sickness and diseases to leave. He exercised His authority as the Son of God. Guess what? You have authority, too! The same power that raised Jesus from the dead is in you. You are a child of God, just like Jesus, and you have authority too. Jesus said, "Speak to your mountains." He didn't say cry and beg me to remove your mountains. He was saying, "Use your authority and speak to your situation like I did." Know who you are in Christ and use your authority!

10. Obedience

"And being found in appearance as a man, He humbled Himself and became obedient to the point of death, even the death of the cross."

Philippians 2:8

Jesus was obedient and surrendered Himself to the will of the Father. Obedience can be hard, it can be scary, it requires lots of faith. But obedience is greatly rewarded. Remember, God doesn't want your sacrifice; He wants your obedience. Obedience brings blessing.

Becoming like Jesus takes time and discipline. Don't get discouraged when you don't act like you should. Humble yourself before The Lord and ask for his help.

Even if you fail today, get yourself back up and keep your eyes on Jesus. Study Him, treasure His words in your heart, and follow His example, and every day, you will be more like Christ. [2]

"So, Jesus said to the Jews who had believed him, "If you abide in my word, you are truly my disciples."

John 8:31

Are you the kind of Christian that is becoming more and more like Jesus?

BECOMING A NEW CREATION

*Therefore, if anyone is in Christ, he is a **new creation**. The old has passed away; behold, the **new** has come.*

2 Corinthians 5:17

God is a Creator. He created the heavens and the earth and everything in them out of nothing. "God said, 'Let there be light,' and there was light." In a similar way, God creates spiritual life and light in the hearts of men, and actually changes the human heart so that it can receive Him.

"And I will give you a new heart, and a new spirit I will put within you. And I will remove the heart of stone from your flesh and give you a heart of flesh."

Ezekiel 36:26

Becoming a new creation occurs by the Spirit of God. The regenerated person believes and is "in Christ" at which point he has become a "new creation."

As we are re-created over the course of our lives, God replaces the old self with a new self and we begin to love and crave the things of the Spirit, and to reject the things that God also rejects.

The people of God are called to be ministers of reconciliation. The purpose is seeking to reconcile, restore and renew. This does nothing to feed us. Rather, it asks us to feed others—even those who should know better and those who have wronged us. The alternative demands we stand under the other and recognize we are all in need of reconciliation.

We cannot take a step toward that call until we first love. Some, no doubt, hear this and think this kind of love is weak. This kind of love gives everyone a pass, tells everyone they are okay or it's cool to be messed up. If any of us think that is what love is, we are mistaken, because none of those things are love.

In many ways, love is violent. However, the violence of love is far different than the violence we dole out to one another every day. The violence of love is what we see on the cross.

The cross was the single greatest act of love in human history, and it was, at the same time, extremely violent. The difference is Jesus took the violence on Himself. He did not strike out at those who mocked Him or fight against those who nailed Him in place; He forgave them. In the midst of punishment at the hands of humans, Jesus loved and loved violently.

The violence of love asks each of us to take the violence on ourselves. It recognizes the brokenness, fear, anger, shame, sin and hate in others and agrees to take all of that on itself. In this, love causes the spiral of violence to cease.

If we are willing to imitate this kind of love, we will find it's quite hard to spend our time judging others. Because if we love others enough to serve them, to not return an insult and let their pain be ours, we will find judgment and punishment no longer fit.

"Judge not, and you will not be judged; condemn not, and you will not be condemned; forgive, and you will be forgiven."

Luke 6:37

Too often, we miss this first step and fail to love.

We as Christians learn to overcome our attitude. We learn that we should not judge others.

"Judge not, that you be not judged. For with the judgment, you pronounce you will be judged, and with the measure you use it will be measured to you."

Matthew 7:1-2

We are all familiar with Jesus' words, "Do not judge."

Why do we so often insist on judging others? We are willing to entertain conversations about most anyone who makes a mistake or does something wrong, even when it has nothing to do with us. Something in us likes to see people pay for their misdeeds. So, we attack.

Our attacks come in the form of opinions, jokes, social media posting and conversations. We call people names, label others, and compete to characterize and make sure others know our thoughts. It's a kind of public punishment that we get to enforce. We launch toxic, crippling words as a way of inflicting harm on those we believe should know better. But it gets even worse.

Conversations abound of how people in the Church cast judgment on others. Yes, we are to discern good from evil, but we insist on judgment as a form of condemnation. It may be the single greatest reason men and women choose to leave the Church altogether. Many people still carry the wounds given to them by others.

We fail to see that our form of judgment and punishment only creates a divide and forces others out. Yet, no matter how often we hear Jesus' words, we just can't seem to stop.

Being a "new creation", we should know better but we continue to struggle with our old self coming back to life. Yet we still retain this judgmental attitude.

Christianity teaches us to love and accept others as they are, without passing judgment. Yet, a common behavior is being overly critical and judgmental.

We too often point out the faults in others, criticize their choices, or look down upon them for not living up to their version of 'Christian standards'. This judgmental attitude directly contradicts the teachings of love, acceptance, and understanding that Christianity stands for.

A true Christian understands that everyone is on their own spiritual journey, with their own struggles and victories. We offer support and guidance, instead of criticism and judgment.

However, a recent George Barna poll revealed that 78% of Americas say that the evangelical church is the most judgmental segment of American society. It should break our hearts to hear this but too many people see Christians as judgmental, and that's because we are.

On one hand, we live in a very wicked world that ought to be judged. But for many non-Christians, Christians have become "Ministers of Condemnation." Rather than reacting to people as God's creation, treating them with mercy and love, we immediately condemn them because of their behavior or beliefs. Yes, we all, at one time or another, been guilty of doing this.

Christians are often pictured as being unloving, judgmental, and narrow-minded because we are known as the ones who often say, "Don't do this and don't do that!"

Sinful people don't like to be told, "Stop It." It's like Christians are throwing cold water upon them and their behaviors. Now, that doesn't mean we should let evil slide by without a word. But there is a big difference between acting as judge and acting like Jesus.

Christians were once known as the people who loved God and loved each other.

Jesus said;

"A new commandment I give to you, that you love one another: just as I have loved you, you also are to love one another. By this all people will know that you are my disciples, if you have love for one another."
John 13:34-35

What happened to our love for one another? Non-Christians are known to look at us and say, "Loving God and loving others! Are you kidding me? I know many Christians who can't even get along with each other."

What's happened to us? Our love for Jesus and for each other can sometimes disappear. Christians are often considered to be judgmental because we have too many hypocrites among us.

Jesus told us to pull the "plank" out of our own eyes before we point to the sin from someone else's eye. 1

Many of us claim to be "self-righteously" judging others, but a person cannot judge self-righteously without sin being involved. We are all sinners as we are born into sin and we all freely commit sins throughout our lives (Romans 3:23). Sin can easily be the reason why we judge others. Self-righteously judging others comes from pride.

The Bible tells us pride is a sin (Proverbs 8:13, 18:12; 1 John 2:16). The original sin was rooted in pride, which ultimately caused disobedience to God. Pride is a common sin for us to fall into due to it being the original sin.

The sin of pride causes us to be obsessed over ourselves, our successes, and our achievements. Pride makes us believe that we are better than others.

When we are tempted to judge others self-righteously, it is time to step back, think, and pray. Being tempted does not mean we have to act on the temptation. Instead, God can help us overcome our temptation.

"No temptation has overtaken you that is not common to man. God is faithful, and he will not let you be tempted beyond your ability, but with the temptation he will also provide the way of escape, that you may be able to endure it."

1 Corinthians 10:13

We must learn to help and love others instead of judging others. If we see a brother or sister in Christ who is caught in a sin, we should help them — not judge them. Judgment is almost never done in love. The only person who judges righteously is the Lord (Psalm 7:11).

It is best to leave all judgment to God. As human beings, we cannot judge others without sin being involved. If someone we know is struggling with drug addiction, alcohol addiction, or any other sin, we should not judge them. Gossiping, speaking badly of them, and thinking less of the individual is not right. If we truly love our neighbor, we will treat them as Jesus would.

The Lord would not judge them and speak maliciously about them. Rather, the Lord would extend love, grace, and compassion. This does not mean that it is okay for the person to commit the sin because it is not.

Instead, it means that we must offer true, loving, and caring help to our brothers and sisters in Christ who are struggling. You can help someone without judging them. Think about how you feel when someone judges you.

Most likely, it makes you feel bad about yourself, and it hurts your feelings. When you judge others, the individual you are judging is also hurt. Think about this the next time you feel like self-righteously judging another person.

There is no pride, hate, or bad intent involved when we love others as Jesus loves us. In fact, Jesus tells us we need to treat others the way we want to be treated (Matthew 7:12; Luke 6:31). If we treat others the way we want to be treated, we are truly obeying God's commands.

Self-righteousness has no place in a believer's life because it is a life of pride. Judging others will only cause pain for us and others. Not to mention the fact that nobody likes a person who judges others and gossips about others behind their back.

No matter what a person has done, it is not our place to judge. All judgment belongs to God because He is the only righteous judge. The Lord wants us to be kind, caring, and compassionate to others, not judgmental, hateful, and prideful.

We are to be Jesus' light to the world, not Jesus' judges of the world.

"There is only one lawgiver and judge, he who is able to save and to destroy. But who are you to judge your neighbor?"
                                                                James 4:12

Thus, do not self-righteously judge others because sin is always involved. 2

Many of us have abandoned our call to be ministers of reconciliation. Rather than renew, redeem and restore, we tear down and create mounds of ruin. We have a bloodlust, forgetting all the while that the blood spilled on the cross was enough for all of us—and no more blood needs to be spilled.

The invitation for each of us is to abandon judgment, to abstain from condemnation, to forego punishment and pursue the violence of love. We must always speak life upon others. It demands that we feed others rather than feed ourselves. Perhaps if we, through the power of the Spirit, can do this, we just might find less judgment. More than that, we will find more reconciliation. 3

Once we learn to stop judging, then we can learn to offer forgiveness.

*"For if you forgive others their trespasses, your heavenly Father will also forgive you, but if you do not forgive others
their trespasses, neither will your Father forgive your trespasses."*
Matthew 6:14-15

Christians have responded to God's offer of forgiveness by making a choice to stop living for themselves and allow God to make them who He wants them to be.

Many people think they must behave a certain way to become a Christian. The Bible explains that becoming a Christian is not about behavior, but about responding to Jesus' offer of forgiveness.

"For by grace you have been saved through faith. And this is not your own doing; it is the gift of God, not a result of works, so that no one may boast."
Ephesians 2:8-9

However, people behave differently after becoming a Christian because their relationship with God changes them. People do good things for many reasons, but a Christian is motivated to do good things because they love God. 4

When we refuse to forgive a wrong, we become part of the problem. When God's people practice forgiveness, sweetness replaces harshness.

We cannot force another to have a spirit of forgiveness, but we can demonstrate it by how we act. It's not always possible to mend a broken relationship. Some people refuse to accept responsibility for what they have done, always blaming someone else for what happened. We must be willing to go the extra mile in an effort to be reconciled with someone who has turned against us, and remember always to pray for them.

A marvelous example of this is revealed in the life of Joseph. His brothers were jealous of him and sold him into slavery. But as the Old Testament story unfolds in Genesis 50, we see that Joseph did not hold it against them. The Lord used Joseph to save his family, and even a whole nation. Because of Joseph's demonstration of forgiveness, he was blessed of God. If we cannot find it in our hearts to forgive within our own family, we will never exhibit this attribute of Christ with others and know God's blessings. [5]

Let's always remember what Jesus said from the cross about those who were crucifying Him:

"And Jesus said, "Father, forgive them, for they know not what they do."

Luke 23:34

C. S. Lewis is quoted as saying, "To be a Christian means to forgive the inexcusable because God has forgiven the inexcusable in you." We are quick to acknowledge the truth of Lewis' words, but how many of us truly live out forgiveness?

We must forgive others because God has forgiven us. Jesus taught us to pray to the Father, "Forgive us our debts, as we forgive our debtors" (Matthew 6:12). Like God, to forgive someone means to no longer hold sin against the person who has sinned against you. When we forgive someone, we are once again in a positive relationship with them.

Forgiving someone does not mean that the offender experiences no consequences for his or her actions. When grievous harm is done, consequences follow. We see this in our relationship with God. If, for example, we were to steal something, the Lord will forgive us if we repent. But that does not mean we will not have to suffer criminal punishment or pay back the person from whom we stole. God forgave David for his sin with Bathsheba, but that sin had severe consequences that followed him the rest of his life in the form of family turmoil (see 2 Samuel). We can and must forgive those who have sinned against us, but when criminal behavior is involved in the sin, it should be reported to the civil authorities, whom God gave to protect us from evildoers (Rom. 13:1–7).

"Judge not, and you will not be judged; condemn not, and you will not be condemned; forgive, and you will be forgiven."

Luke 6:37

Someone who comes to you and asks for forgiveness is showing a sign of repentance. We should never withhold forgiveness from someone who asks for it from us (see Matthew 18:21, 22; Luke 17:3). If we do not forgive someone who asks, we do not display the richness of God's mercy to us in Jesus Christ (see Matthew 18:23–35).

Sin is a sad reality of life in a fallen world, and it has major consequences. Jesus Christ willingly gave His life for our sins. Our forgiveness came at an unimaginable price. The beauty of the Christian life is that we can forgive others in a way that God has forgiven us. 6

What if you struggle with the ability to forgive others?

A real Christian knows that forgiveness isn't just about the other person; it's also about finding peace within themselves. They understand the power of forgiveness in mending relationships and fostering love and understanding.

Many people also struggle with the ability to forgive themselves. I have seen this often in prison ministry. After imprisonment many inmates hit rock bottom. They exam their lives and focus on their mistakes. Their guilt and shame overpower their emotions and they see themselves as less than human. They know of the hurt they have done to others and they are helpless to do anything about it. They become convinced that they are so bad that it is impossible for them to ever be forgiven.

Self-forgiveness is not about letting yourself off the hook, nor is it a sign of weakness. The act of forgiveness, whether you are forgiving yourself or someone who has wronged you, does not suggest that you are condoning the behavior. To forgive yourself you must realize that God still loves you. He loves you the same before the act and after the act. God's love never changes. God's love is greater than your mistake. Nothing a person can do is so bad that it is more powerful than God's love. God's love always triumphs. It is the strongest known force in the universe, in the heavens or in the earth. Nothing can defeat God's love. Once you can grasp upon this reality, you can learn to not only forgive yourself but to also forgive others. God's love is the first and most important thing you should grasp and hold on to but there are other things you should do. You need to understand your emotions. You need to accept responsibility for what happened and treat yourself with kindness and compassion. You should express remorse for your mistakes and make amends and apologize (including apologizing to yourself) for what has happened. You should look for ways to learn from the experience and you should focus on making better choices in the future.

Forgiveness means that you accept the behavior, you accept what has happened, and you are willing to move past it and move on with your life without reliving your past mistakes. You cannot change the past but you can put it behind you.

Real Christians my find it difficult to forgive someone but eventually they do.

Are you still in chains to the person who has hurt you? Would you like to be free from the bitterness that is binding you and preventing you from moving forward in your life? Take some time right now to admit to God that you have been hurt. Go ahead and acknowledge to the Lord that the person who hurt you owes you for what they have done to you. Then confess any desires for revenge you may have felt, and pray along these lines:

"Lord, I choose to forgive (name of person) for (list what the person did that hurt you) even though it made me feel (painful memories or feelings).

"Whether your offender is sorry or not, whether he ever expresses remorse or not, your decision to release him of his offense and debt to you will release you from your prison of bitterness and enable you to move forward."

"Pay attention to yourselves! If your brother sins, rebuke him, and if he repents, forgive him, and if he 'sins' against you seven times in the day, and turns to you seven times, saying, 'I repent,' you must forgive him."

Luke 17:3-4

Being a "new-creation" helps us overcome the bad habits of judging and un-forgiveness. We know that this new birth was brought about by the will of God. We did not inherit the new nature from our parents or decide to re-create ourselves anew. Neither did God simply clean up our old nature; He created something entirely fresh and unique. The new creation is completely new, brought about from nothing. Only the Creator could accomplish such a feat.

Second, "old things have passed away." The "old" refers to everything that is part of our old nature—natural pride, love of sin, reliance on works, and our former opinions, habits and passions. Most significantly, what we loved has passed away, especially the supreme love of self and with-it self-righteousness, self-promotion, and self-justification. The new creature looks outwardly toward Christ instead of inwardly toward self. The old things died, nailed to the cross with our sin nature.

Old, dead things are replaced with new things, full of life and the glory of God. The newborn soul delights in the things of God and hates the things of the world and the flesh. Our purposes, feelings, desires, and understandings are fresh and different. We see the world differently. The Bible seems to be a new book, and though we may have read it before, there is a beauty about it which we never saw before, and which we wonder at not having perceived. The whole face of nature seems to us to be changed, and we seem to be in a new world. The heavens and the earth are filled with new wonders, and all things seem now to speak forth the praise of God. There are new feelings toward all people—a new kind of love toward family and friends, a new compassion never before felt for enemies, and a new love for all mankind. The things we once loved, we now detest. The sin we once held onto, we now desire to put away forever. We "put off the old man with his deeds" (Colossians 3:9), and put on the "new self, created to be like God in true righteousness and holiness" (Ephesians 4:24).

No one reaches sinless perfection in this life, but the redeemed Christian is being sanctified (made holy) day by day, sinning less and hating it more each time he fails. Yes, we still sin, but unwillingly and less and less frequently as we mature. Our new creation hates the sin that still has a hold on us. The difference is that the new creation is no longer a slave to sin, as we formerly were. We are now freed from sin and it no longer has power over us (Romans 6:6-7). Now we are empowered by and for righteousness. We now have the choice to "let sin reign" or to count ourselves "dead to sin but alive to God in Christ Jesus" (Romans 6:11-12). Best of all, now we have the power to choose. The new creation is a wondrous thing, formed in the mind of God and created by His power and for His glory.

Being a "new creation" can be summarized with the following points:

1. **Spiritual Rebirth**:
   The concept of being a new creation in Christ Jesus begins with a spiritual rebirth. This rebirth is not a physical transformation but a spiritual awakening that occurs when an individual accepts Jesus Christ as their Lord and Savior. It involves a profound change in the person's relationship with God, marking the beginning of a new life in Christ.

2. **Renewed Mindset and Heart**:
   As a new creation, one experiences a renewal of the mind and heart. This renewal involves a shift in perspective, priorities, and desires. The things that once held paramount importance may lose their grip, while a newfound love for God and others becomes the driving force behind one's thoughts and actions.

3. **Freedom from the Old Self**:
   Being a new creation in Christ Jesus signifies freedom from the bondage of sin and the old self. It involves letting go of past mistakes, regrets, and any behavior that is contrary to God's will. This freedom allows individuals to embrace their new identity and live in the fullness of God's grace.

4. **Identity in Christ**:
   Central to the concept of being a new creation is the understanding of one's identity in Christ. This identity is rooted in the truth of being a beloved child of God, forgiven and redeemed through the sacrifice of Jesus. Embracing this identity empowers individuals to live with confidence, knowing that they are deeply loved and accepted by God.

5. **A New Purpose and Calling**:
   As a new creation, individuals are called to live out God's purposes for their lives. This may involve serving others, sharing

the message of hope and redemption, and living in a way that reflects the character of Christ. The new purpose and calling bring meaning and fulfillment to life as believers align themselves with God's plans for the world.

In essence, being a new creation in Christ Jesus encompasses a profound spiritual transformation that redefines one's identity, purpose, and way of living. It is a journey of growth, renewal, and empowerment as individuals embrace the fullness of God's love and grace in their lives. 7

Are you the "New Creation" kind of Christian or the old self Christian?

NEW PRIORITIES

And do not seek what you will eat and what you will drink, and do not keep worrying. For all these things the nations of the world eagerly seek; but your 'Father' knows that you need these things. But seek His kingdom, and these things will be added to you.

Luke 12:29-31

What are your priorities?

As a "new creation" we learn to always put God first! Above society, above political parties, above oneself. It may not be easy but we eventually do.

Johann Wolfgang von Goethe said, "Things which matter most must never be at the mercy of things which matter least."

It's about putting "first things first."

The Bible sets priorities that lead to eternal life. The Word of God tells us that it is vital to put our priorities in the right order and then carefully cultivate each one with zeal and enthusiasm.

Consider three of the most important eternal Christian priorities:

No. 1: God must come first!

When God gave the Ten Commandments at Mount Sinai, He thundered these words: "I am the LORD your God, who brought you out of the land of Egypt, out of the house of bondage. You shall have no other gods before Me" (Exodus 20:2-3).

God does not want us to place anything before Him. His desire is that we worship Him and Him alone. He must come first in our lives.

The Bible tells the story of two sisters, Mary and Martha, who were loyal friends of Jesus Christ. When Christ visited them, they wanted to serve Him in the way each considered was most important. Let's pick up the story:

Now as they went on their way, Jesus entered a village. And a woman named Martha welcomed him into her house. And she had a sister called Mary, who sat at the Lord's feet and listened to his teaching. But Martha was distracted with much serving. And she went up to him and said, "Lord, do you not care that my sister has left me to serve alone? Tell her then to help me." But the Lord answered her, "Martha, Martha, you are anxious and troubled about many things, but one thing is necessary. Mary has chosen the good portion, which will not be taken away from her."

Luke 10:38-42

Serving others is highly important and to be like Christ we must serve others. However, in this instance priorities were an issue. Listening to Christ's teachings was even more important than food preparation. God must always come first.

"For this is the love of God, that we keep His commandments. And His commandments are not burdensome"

1 John 5:3

The evidence that we love God is our striving to keep His commandments.

"Whoever says "I know him" but does not keep his commandments is a liar, and the truth is not in him, but

whoever keeps his word, in him truly the love of God is perfected. By this we may know that we are in him:

1 John 2:4-5

We have to be honest with ourselves. Are we putting our personal relationship with God first, or are we allowing other aspects of our lives to come before the worship of the true God?

The Bible records an incident in which Peter, James and John, who Christ was calling to become His disciples, had their priorities right:

"And when they had brought their boats to land, they left everything and followed him."

Luke 5:11

On the other hand, the Bible records examples of people who had distorted priorities, and who actually rejected Christ's offer to become one of His disciples. Read Luke 9:57-62. Apparently, physical comfort and prosperity were of greater importance to some. For others, taking care of family matters was more crucial than supporting Christ in preaching the gospel.

None of their excuses were of themselves wrong. Is it wrong to stay with a father until he dies or to devote an extended period of time to saying farewell to family members? Certainly not! However, Christ was teaching an important lesson: God was not first in their priorities.

Frequently it is difficult to choose between the affairs of this world and Christ's teachings. Christ stated:

"If anyone comes to me and does not hate his own father and mother and wife and children and brothers and sisters, yes, and even his own life, he cannot be my disciple. Whoever does not bear his own cross and come after me cannot be my disciple."

Luke 14:26-27

Christ did not mean we should stop caring for each member of our family. He was simply teaching that we are to put Him first in our lives. Leaving God out of our planning is unwise (James 4:13-16).

Remember Christ's words: "No one who puts his hand to the plow and looks back is fit for the kingdom of God."

Luke 9:62

Once we have set following Christ as our top priority, there is no going back (Hebrews 10:37-39).

This leads us to our second Christian priority:

No. 2: Develop a godly, righteous character.

What is godly, righteous character? A well-known educator in religious matters, Herbert W. Armstrong, wrote the following definition of perfect character: "It is the ability, in a separate entity with free moral agency, to come to the knowledge of the right from the wrong—the true from the false—and to choose the right, and possess the will to enforce self-discipline to do the right and resist the wrong" (The Incredible Human Potential, p. 138; see more about Mr. Armstrong in our article "The Church: A Worldwide Work").

In his book The Death of Character, James Davison Hunter wrote: "Does character really matter? The collective wisdom of the ages would say it matters a great deal. In both classical and biblical cultures—civilizations that have been so deeply formative to our own—people well understood there to be a direct association between the character of individuals and the well-being of the society as a whole. Individual character was essential to decency, order, and justice within public life. Without it, hardship was not far off. ... Indeed, much of the history of the ancient Hebrews can be told as a story of blessing for faithfulness to God—abiding by God's standard of holiness—and punishment for abandoning those standards" (p. 4).

Mr. Hunter cites Deuteronomy 30:15-19 as support for his statements.

With our new priorities we learn to focus on God's will over our will. When it comes to important decisions, God's will now takes priority in our lives.

The apostle Paul admonished Christians to "be transformed by the renewing of your mind, that you may prove what is that good and acceptable and perfect will of God" (Romans 12:2).

To be led by the will of God is to embody the character of God—to become more like God. Christ set the perfect example.

Christ taught His followers to pray often that God's Kingdom be established, and that "Your [the Father's] will be done on earth as it is in heaven" (Matthew 6:10). Jesus said;

"For I have come down from heaven, not to do my own will but the will of him who sent me."

John 6:38

Even when faced with a horrifying trial of physical pain and mental torment, Christ prayed, "Not My will, but Yours, be done" (Luke 22:42).

Overcoming our selfish nature and replacing it with God's character should be uppermost in our minds. As Christ taught:

"You therefore must be perfect, as your heavenly Father is perfect."

Matthew 5:48

No. 3: Seek first the Kingdom of God

In His Sermon on the Mount, Christ taught some of the most meaningful principles of Christian living in the entire Bible (Matthew 5-7). One of these is:

"But seek first the kingdom of God and His righteousness, and all these things shall be added to you."
Matthew 6:33

This verse not only summarizes the first two priorities, focusing on God and His righteousness—but it brings to our attention the importance of the Kingdom of God. 1

What is the Kingdom of God?

It is the perfect and just government of God that will be established over the earth at the return of Christ, when

"The kingdoms of this world have become the kingdoms of our Lord and of His Christ, and He shall reign forever and ever!"
Revelation 11:15

The fourth and final Christian priority;

No. 4: Proclaim the excellencies of God to others.
God has called us out of the world as His people so that we can go back into the world and proclaim the excellencies of Him who called us out of darkness into His marvelous light.

Gathered as the church, we worship our great God by proclaiming His excellencies to one another and we build up one another. Scattered into the world, we proclaim God's mercy and light to those who are still in the darkness.

It would be great to think that everyone who doesn't know God would be responsive and want to believe. Some are; but the Bible is clear that we can expect some to reject not only the message, but also us. Jesus is very controversial in today's society and some will be offended. If so, we shouldn't blast people with God's judgment. Our

Savior was kind to sinners and yet He spoke plainly about sin and judgment. We should always be gracious.

"Let your speech always be gracious, seasoned with salt, so that you may know how you ought to answer each person."

Colossians 4:6

But we must remember that the biblical Christ is going to offend many people, for at least two reasons:

First, the cross of Christ is offensive.

"But we preach Christ crucified, a stumbling block to Jews and folly to Gentiles."

1 Corinthians 1:23

The cross humbles human pride. It tells people that their own good works will not get them into heaven. It tells them that they are sinners who have offended a holy God. People don't like that.

Second, Christ's lordship offends people.

Everyone likes the idea of an Aladdin's genie-Jesus, who will fulfill their desires. But a Christ who is Lord, who confronts sin and demands obedience--that's another story! If you proclaim Christ crucified and Christ as Lord, some will believe and be saved. But others will reject Him and you. Be prepared!

Believing or not believing in Jesus Christ separates people into two distinct camps. Believers are joined to God and His people and one day will be exalted with Christ in heaven. Unbelievers who do not repent are in the darkness, headed for God's judgment. Jesus Christ is the central issue in belief or unbelief. Either He is the corner stone on whom a person puts his faith and builds his life; or, He is a stone of stumbling and rock of offense over which a person falls.

What does Peter mean when he says that unbelievers "stumble because they are disobedient to the word, and to this they were also appointed? Are some appointed to perish? Peter's purpose here is to encourage believers under persecution. Thus, his point is that the raging of the wicked is under God's sovereign control, so that believers need not fear.

"Why do the nations rage and the peoples plot in vain? The kings of the earth set themselves, and the rulers take counsel together, against the Lord and against his Anointed, saying, "Let us burst their bonds apart and cast away their cords from us." He who sits in the heavens laughs; the Lord holds them in derision. Then he will speak to them in his wrath, and terrify them in his fury, saying, "As for me, I have set my King on Zion, my holy hill."

Psalm 2:1-6

Jesus will someday be glorified in His saving His elect and in justly condemning the reprobate. We are assured that the wicked will be punished.

And yet, those who are disobedient are responsible for their sin, even if it is in line with God's predestined plan.

"This Jesus, delivered up according to the definite plan and foreknowledge of God, you crucified and killed by the hands of lawless men."

Acts 2:23

But they need not remain in disobedience and rebellion. God offers them mercy and forgiveness if they will turn to Christ.

"For God has consigned all to disobedience, that he may have mercy on all."

Romans 11:32

No one has piled up more sin than God's mercy can cover. Christ's death is sufficient for the chief of sinners. All may come and receive mercy at the cross.

Let's us all take this opportunity to reexamine our priorities. First and foremost, have you truly believed in Christ as Savior and Lord? Is He and His death on the cross precious to you? If so, is He central in your life? Are you coming continually to Him and building your life on Him? Are you offering your life as a spiritual sacrifice to Him? Are you seeking to be built together with His people or do you just attend church? You may need to commit yourself to a local church. Are you seeking to proclaim His excellencies to those in darkness, that they, too, may come to know the Savior?

These are the priorities we should have as God's people who have received His mercy. 2

Become the kind of Christian that learns to focus on priorities and put "first things first". Put God at the very top of your priority list today!

DISCOVERING OUR PURPOSE

"For we are God's handiwork, created in Christ Jesus to do good works, which God prepared in advance for us to do."

Ephesians 2:10

What is your purpose in life?

Have you ever thought about what your purpose is as a Christian? It's a question that can spark curiosity and maybe even a bit of confusion. But here's the good news: your purpose isn't hidden away in some far-off place. It's right here, within your reach. As it says in Ephesians, we are created in Christ Jesus to do good works.

Living purposefully as a Christian means pursuing God's unique calling for your life daily. It requires looking inward to assess your motivations, gifts, and passions to understand how God equipped you for Kingdom work. It also requires looking outward to study the needs in the world, seek wise counsel, and step out in faith.

So, how can we practically apply biblical principles to live with intention each day in the specific way God created us? There are seven keys we can explore based on scripture to help illuminate our path as we seek to discover our God-given calling and purpose.

1. Understand Your Identity in Christ

The foundation for living a purposeful Christian life is understanding your true identity in Christ. When you placed your faith in Jesus as Savior, you became a new creation (2 Corinthians 5:17). Your core identity changed from sinner to saint, from separated from God to His beloved child.

This new identity shapes every aspect of our purpose and encompasses profound truths including:

- We are loved unconditionally by God (Romans 8:38-39).

- We are saved by grace, not by our effort (Ephesians 2:8-9).

- We have direct access to the Father as His child (Ephesians 2:18).

- We are joint heirs with Christ, sharing in His inheritance (Romans 8:17).

- God delights in us and sings over us (Zephaniah 3:17).

- We are complete in Christ, lacking nothing (Colossians 2:10).

- We are chosen, holy, and dearly loved by God (Colossians 3:12).

Meditating on these truths floods them into the core of our being. We gain confidence that we belong to Him and have inherent worth. This frees us from striving or basing our value on worldly approval. Our calling flows from who we are, not what we do. A firm grasp on our identity in Christ is the foundation for living out our purpose with boldness.

Let your identity in Christ be your perspective on work, relationships, ministry, and everything in between.

2. Connect with God Through Prayer and Scripture

Once we understand our identity in Christ, nurturing an intimate relationship with God is essential for living out our purpose. Set aside regular time to connect with your Heavenly Father through prayer and studying the Bible.

Bring your heart before God in prayer, openly sharing your thoughts, needs, fears, and desires. Praise Him for His blessings and character. Confess any sins that could hinder your connection. Pray for wisdom and direction each morning before starting your day. Developing a dynamic prayer life shows your reliance on God rather than yourself.

Immersing yourself in Scripture renews your mind and transforms you into Christ's image (Romans 12:2). Ask the Holy Spirit to speak truth to you as you read God's Word. Take time to meditate on verses that encourage and challenge you. The Bible equips you for every good work God has called you to do (2 Timothy 3:16-17). As you abide in Scripture, your thoughts and actions align more with God's purposes.

Scheduling consistent time to practice spiritual disciplines demonstrates that connecting with God is a priority over the distractions of life. Devote yourself to pursuing closeness with the Lord every day. Your calling flows out of your intimacy with Him.

3. Listen to the Stirrings of Your Heart

God placed passions, motivations, and gifts within you for a reason – to equip you for the good works He prepared for you (Ephesians 2:10). Pay attention to the desires and burdens He has placed on your heart. The things that stir you up, that you think about frequently or feel strongly about, often indicate areas where God wants to use you. Your reactions and experiences also shape your unique passions. Make sure your heart falls in line with God's teaching. If it does, you can trust where God is leading you in your purpose.

Perhaps you have a burden for the homeless because of struggles you or your family faced. Or you love music and long to lead others in worship. The impressions God leaves can become beautiful threads woven into the tapestry of your purpose.

What burdens weigh on your heart? Are you troubled by poverty, hunger, injustice, or other issues in society? Often God stirs a holy discontentment around a specific need, motivating you to act. Turn the passions and burdens God instilled in you into prayer and Spirit-led action.

We should also present our desires to God.

"Commit your work to the Lord, and your plans will be established."
Proverbs 16:3

Listen for God's guidance. Let Him prune away distractions and confirm which stirrings align with the good works He has prepared for you. Then courageously take steps to follow where He leads.

As you tune your ear to the stirrings in your heart, write down the desires, burdens, and talents God reveals. Ask Him to align your heart more fully with His purposes. Then boldly yet wisely follow as God directs your steps in cultivating and applying your unique blend of gifts and passions. God has crafted you for a unique calling. Listen for His whisper, follow His lead. Your life will blossom with meaning when you live out His plan.

4. Serve Others with Your Gifts

God carefully crafted you with specific talents, abilities, and experiences to carry out the good works He prepared for you (Ephesians 2:10). Take stock of all the skills and knowledge you've gained so far through education, jobs, hobbies, volunteer work, and overcoming challenges.

Make a comprehensive list of your capabilities and acquired wisdom – these become tools in finding your purpose. Reflect on the ways God has uniquely shaped you through triumphs and hardships. Your story has equipped you with compassion and insights to help others who are now facing similar seasons.

By taking inventory of all God has entrusted to you, you gain a clearer picture of the gifts and resources available to direct toward serving others. These gifts are not yours to keep but to give faithfully to others and for Kingdom impact.

Use Your Gifts to Meet Practical Needs. Look for ways to direct your gifts towards meeting practical needs around you. Do you enjoy organizing? Help declutter homes for the elderly. Are you great at DIY projects? Serve a single mom by repairing things around her house. Your gifts can meet emotional and spiritual needs too. Send encouraging notes to those going through hard times. Visit someone struggling with loneliness.

"As each has received a gift, use it to serve one another, as good stewards of God's varied grace."

1 Peter 4:10

Be a Faithful Steward. Don't bury your talents but use them. As you serve others in your sweet spot of skills and interests, you'll often experience great joy and fulfillment.

Listen to God's Guidance. Listen for where God leads you to best invest your unique blend of gifts. Be ready to step out of your comfort zone and watch how He stretches your abilities beyond what you thought possible. The more your gifts are used, the more they will grow.

5. Take Challenges as Opportunities

Walking in your God-given purpose doesn't mean avoiding hardships or trials. In fact, some of the most significant opportunities to grow in your calling come wrapped in challenges. How you respond to difficulties determines whether they derail you or develop you.

When obstacles arise, take a step back to pray and reflect. Ask God to show you what lessons He wants you to learn and how to strengthen your character and calling. Remind yourself of biblical truths – God's sovereignty, His presence with you, and His promise to work all things for good (Romans 8:28).

Lean into the Christian Community. Lean into the support of the Christian community during struggles. God often uses the encouragement of others to lift and sustain us. Be willing to be humble and vulnerable by sharing your needs.

See God's Faithfulness. Challenges develop endurance and deep trust in God's faithfulness. As you see His goodness through stormy seasons, you gain the courage to take bolder steps of faith. With God's help, you'll reflect back one day grateful for the fruits cultivated through the darkest nights.

When you encounter inevitable hardships and trials, prayerfully reflect on how God may want to use them for growth and refinement. Consider the following ways challenges can become opportunities:

Financial hardship challenge: Opportunity to deepen trust in God's provision and cultivate wisdom in stewardship.

Health challenge: Opportunity to rely more fully on God's strength, develop empathy for others suffering, and reorder priorities.

Relational challenge: Opportunity to practice forgiveness, see from other's perspectives, and grow in loving others.

Work challenge: Opportunity to reflect on aligned vocational calling, cultivate perseverance and creativity, and explore new possibilities.

Failure or setback challenge: Opportunity for humbling, to identify lessons learned, and to lean wholly on God's grace and redemptive power.

God can use any challenge or trial for good by transforming it into an opportunity for growth. Ask God to show you what He wants to develop in you. Then courageously walk through the door of opportunity He opens.

6. Stay Patient and Trust in God's Timing

Discovering and living out your God-given purpose requires yielding to God's timetable, not demanding your own. His ways are higher than ours (Isaiah 55:9). What He cares about most is your continual growth in Christ-like character and deepening intimacy with Him. That requires cultivating patience.

Surrender Your Timeline. When eager to see forward progress in an area of calling, bring your desire before God. Surrender your timeline and humble yourself under His sovereignty. Choose to trust in His perfect wisdom and timing over your limited human understanding.

God Uses Waiting Seasons. God often uses waiting seasons to prepare you for what He has prepared. While impatient, we may rush ahead of God's timing and miss His intended blessings. Or we try manufacturing outcomes rather than waiting for God's nudging. But abiding in Christ and waiting on the Lord renews strength and clarity of vision (Isaiah 40:31).

Remain faithful in small things while waiting for God's direction. Focus on growing your gifts and serving where you can. Keep your focus on God rather than your desires. Let your purpose be about God's purpose. As you wait on the Lord, He will bring forth His calling in His perfect way and time.

7. Live a Life of Gratitude

Cultivating a heart of gratitude fuels you to passionately pursue your calling and purpose day after day. Thankfulness shifts your focus from dissatisfaction with your current situation to awe of how God is working. Rather than getting lost in what you lack, you become aware of just how much you have been given.

Start by giving thanks for your salvation and identity in Christ. Thank God for His unconditional love and the grace that equips you to live for His glory.

Give thanks for the people who have helped you along your journey and the community walking alongside you. See the gifts in those around you and take time to affirm them. Be grateful for opportunities to use your gifts and make a difference, no matter how small. Thank God for the work He is doing in and through you. Find small gifts to give thanks for.

"Give thanks in all circumstances; for this is the will of God in Christ Jesus for you."

1 Thessalonians 5:18

Gratitude fuels joy and keeps your eyes open to God's daily blessings along the path of purpose He has you on. Overflowing thankfulness to God enables you to stay faithful. With a heart of praise, you'll be motivated for new adventures.

Discovering your God-given purpose requires an ongoing journey of seeking God's heart day by day. There will be mountaintop moments of joy and valley seasons of difficulty alike. Through it all, hold tightly to your identity in Christ.

"And I am sure of this, that he who began a good work in you will bring it to completion at the day of Jesus Christ."

Philippians 1:6

Draw strength from His Word and Spirit living within you. You have all you need to faithfully walk out you're calling and make a Kingdom impact. God is with you! 1

These seven keys will help you discover your calling. It certainly did for me. The first thing I discovered is that my calling was a challenge to my personality. I have always seen myself as shy and a little unsociable. Speaking with others is not my favorite thing to do. I often become nervous and fearful that I would say something foolish so I have always felt more comfortable listening and not on talking.

I learned many years ago that my spiritual gift is encouragement and empathy. Because of my shyness and fear I hide this gift for too many years. After going many years being ashamed for not using my gift, I finally felt the nudge to take a risk and get out of my comfort zone. God called me clearly to act and put my fear behind me. It wasn't easy, and yes, I felt very nervous and uncomfortable, but I finally took a step. I made the decision to let God be in control and I submitted to His calling in my life. And now a person like me with very few words of my own, is able to help others in need by words of encouragement and prayer. The Holy Spirit gives me the words to encourage others. I can sometimes still feel unsure of myself but when I take the step to help others, the Holy Spirit is always there to provide the right words for me to say as long as I am obedient and focus on listening and hearing His words.

One thing I have learned is that when encouraging others, I have felt the most amazing blessing I have ever encountered. The joy I receive when helping others has uplifted my soul and spirit in a way I could have never imaged. I have never felt the presence of the Holy Spirit more powerfully inside me as I do when I pray for others. I now look forward to opportunities of encouraging and praying for others. An yet I let so many years just slip away. Please don't make the same mistake I did. Find you gift and take it seriously. Put it to good use.

The other thing I have learned is that God does not call the qualified, He qualifies the called. God doesn't use perfect people; He uses faithful people. If He can use me, He can also use you. You do have a calling. I know every Christian has a calling. Every Christian has a gift(s) from God that they can use to help others. We all have the capacity to help others because it all comes from God. Many other Christians like me have had problems with anxiety and fear, and they too learned to get past this and have since become amazing servants of God. God knows what He is doing and He knows exactly how to use us all. God is asking for us to abandon our comfort zone. So, let me ask, how can God use you?

"And we know that in all things God works for the good of those who love him, who have been called according to his purpose."

Romans 8:28

Become the kind of Christian that discovers your purpose and use it to help others!

ABANDONING OUR COMFORT ZONE

"Have I not commanded you? Be strong and courageous. Do not be afraid; do not be discouraged, for the Lord your God will be with you wherever you go."

Joshua 1:9

Are you stuck in your comfort zone?

As Christians we must continue to "grow in the grace and knowledge of our Lord and Savior Jesus Christ" (2 Peter 3:18). Jesus did not call us to be fans, He called us to be participants. He calls us to deny ourselves, take up our crosses, and follow Him (Luke 9:23). All Christians go through seasons of greater and lesser growth, but there is always an upward move toward God. It may at times be two steps forward and one step back, but there will be progress. If we continue in the same worldly mindset we had before conversion, chances are that we were never really converted at all. A real Christian is one who looks to Christ for instructions. A real Christian yearns to be more like Jesus and rids his or her life of distractions, temptations, and obstacles to that goal. When God adopts us as His children, He desires that we take on the family resemblance.

For those whom he foreknew he also predestined to be conformed to the image of his Son, in order that he might be the firstborn among many brothers.

Romans 8:29

A true Christian will look more and more like their Savior. We must take action...we must get out of our comfort zone. How do we know that God Is calling us all to get out of your comfort zone?

1. Do you feel stuck in your current season?

If your life has been stuck in an unwanted season for a Long time, this Is most likely a sign God wants you to get out of your comfort zone.

If God wanted to create a bunch of mindless robots that are simply preprogrammed to do exactly what He wanted, He would have done this. But that is obviously not what God has done. God created us to be partners with Him in the decisions we make in life. Yes, God is ultimately in control and reserves the sovereign right to allow or not allow certain things to happen; but much of what happens in our lives is also directly connected to our willingness to follow the Spirit's leading.

God will often tell you what He wants you to do but then leave the choice to do it up to you. When we choose to not do something that God wants us to do, oftentimes the result is a lack of progression in life. God won't make you do certain things; but if you refuse to follow where He's leading, He will let you remain stuck right where you are.

This principle can be seen in the life of Jonah. When God called Jonah to preach to Nineveh, Jonah refused, God caused him to literally get stuck in life, unable to move forward. God did not cause the fish to swim to Nineveh to then force Jonah to do what He wanted, but God did hold him in the belly of the fish until he repented of his refusal to follow God.

Those who pay regard to vain idols forsake their hope of steadfast love. But I with the voice of thanksgiving will sacrifice to you; what I have vowed I will pay. Salvation belongs to the Lord!" And the Lord spoke to the fish, and it vomited Jonah out upon the dry land.

Jonah 2:8-10

Likewise, if you are stuck in an unwanted season of life because you are refusing to do something God wants you to do, you will remain stuck until you get out of your comfort zone and obey God's call on your life.

2. Do you fear taking a step of faith?

If your fear of taking a step of faith is causing more anxiety than the worst-case scenario, this is often a sign God wants you to get out of your comfort zone.

When we let our minds think too much about taking a step of faith rather than just taking that step of faith, the fear that can start to build up inside of us can actually then start to surpass the original fears we had. In other words, when you think too much about something you already know you should do, you are just allowing unnecessary anxiety to build up in you. If you know what God is telling you to do, sitting there and thinking about it just causes an unnecessary paralysis by analysis.

If illogical fears and anxieties are growing inside you as you wait to get out of your comfort zone, you will sense God calling you more and more. The best thing you can do is act when you sense God telling you to act. Thinking too much about the worst-case scenario often creates more fear than the actual worst-case scenario could truly produce. Our negative thoughts often create more issues for us than if we just did what we were called to do. Even if it goes horribly wrong, it is often not as bad as suffering with endless internal anxiety.

Do you often wonder "What if?" What are the positives and the negatives of taking the action we are called to do? Not taking action will cause unrest in your soul, while taking the action could lead to either failure or success. If you fail, so what! At least you tried. It's certainly not the end of the world. We all fail at one time or another. But what if you succeed? Imagine the blessing and sense of accomplishment you will receive. The reward is just too great to pass up. Just go for it!

Finally, brothers, whatever is true, whatever is honorable, whatever is just, whatever is pure, whatever is lovely, whatever is commendable, if there is any excellence, if there is anything worthy of praise, think about these things. What you have learned and received and heard and seen in me—practice these things, and the God of peace will be with you.

Philippians 4:8-9

According this passage, we must dwell on holy thoughts and we must then put into practice the lessons God is teaching us. If we allow ourselves to think about our fears and we never put into practice what God is teaching us, we will regret never getting out of our comfort zones. You are never blessed in the boat...you must get out of the boat to walk on water!

3. Do You Get Mad at Yourself for Being too Passive?
This Is often a sign the Holy Spirit Is convicting you to get out of your comfort zone.

This may be the worst part of being too passive in life. The fact that you miss out on so much good that you could have experienced but instead are confined to the prison of your own mind as you feel the pain of your own inactivity.

One of the lessons we can learn from the story about Jesus and the young rich man. Jesus pinpointed this man's greatest stronghold in his life – his possessions.

And Jesus, looking at him, loved him, and said to him, "You lack one thing: go, sell all that you have and give to the poor, and you will have treasure in heaven; and come, follow me." Disheartened by the saying, he went away sorrowful, for he had great possessions.

Mark 10:21-22

In love, Jesus will point out that "one thing" in our lives which we are passively withholding from Him. This man was ready to follow Jesus, but Jesus knew there was a fear in him that would prevent his true obedience. For this man it was his possessions. For others it is relationships, safety, or earthly prestige. Whatever it is, Jesus will always point it out in love.

If you turn from Jesus and His calling, you will walk away disheartened and sorrowful. Imagine what the years after looked like for this young rich man? Imagine how he must have felt whenever he thought back to that day when he refused to follow Jesus because he chose to remain in his comfort-zone?

If you often get upset with yourself for missing opportunities you sensed God was leading you to take, this is often a sign the Lord is telling you it's time to get out of your comfort zone.

4. Is the Risk Worth the Possible Reward?

This is another sign God is leading you out of your comfort zone.

God will not call us just to make dangerous decision in life. There are many times where we will want to take a risk but God will tell us not to. God is not against safety and wisdom.

However, God will often present us with risks that are worth it because of what is at stake. You will know God wants you to get out of your comfort zone and into the unknown when the risk is truly worth the reward.

As Jesus said, "*Whoever finds his life will lose it, and whoever loses his life for my sake will find it.*"

Matthew 10:39

It can be a scary thing to give up your life to follow Jesus. But the risk is certainly worth the reward. 1

"Then he said to them all: 'Whoever wants to be my disciple must deny themselves and take up their cross daily and follow me.'"

Luke 9:23

Are you the kind of Christian still stuck in your comfort zone, or the kind of Christian that has escaped your comfort zone?

SERVING AND GIVING

"For I was hungry and you gave me food, I was thirsty and you gave me drink, I was a stranger and you welcomed me, I was naked and you clothed me, I was sick and you visited me, I was in prison and you came to me. Truly I tell you, whatever you did for one of the least of these brothers and sisters of mine, you did for me."

Matthew 25:35-40

Why is serving so important?
"For even the Son of Man came not to be served but to serve, and to give His life as a ransom for many."

Mark 10:45

It's all about serving! Jesus came to serve and as followers of Jesus we must also learn to serve others!

"For you were called to freedom, brothers. Only do not use your freedom as an opportunity for the flesh, but through love serve one another."

Galatians 5:13

We must serve everyone, even the least of these!

And the King will answer them, 'Truly, I say to you, as you did it to one of the least of these my brothers, you did it to me.'

Matthew 25:40

Giving and serving may be one of the most overlooked job descriptions of a Christian. It seems too simple yet few believers serve others. Many Christians spend most of their lives faithfully attending church on a regular basis but fail to serve others or even volunteer at their local church or in their community. Christians are not called to sit in the bleachers, we must participate on the field. Authentic Christians hear the calling and obey the call of the Lord.

This is what true faith and religion is all about. James put it succinctly when he wrote,

Religion that is pure and undefiled before God the Father is this: to visit orphans and widows in their affliction, and to keep oneself unstained from the world.

James 1:27

Do you visit church members in the hospital? Do you visit people in the nursing homes? Do you visit people in prison?

We're not just talking about your immediate family. How do you serve those you don't even know?

Seniors in nursing homes can be considered orphans. Sixty percent never receive any visitors at all. We know that there are many widows but there are also many widowers there too.

God is pleased with us when we visit them. God is pleased when we visit the lonely. They are not only physical orphans but spiritual ones too. James did not specify what age these orphans and widows would be. Why wouldn't God be pleased when we serve and visit them?

Visiting those in hospitals, nursing homes, or even those in prison is part of what James (and God) calls pure religion. This is the meat and potatoes of Christianity. God is a Father to the fatherless. He is a defender of the widows and widowers. God is not interested in religion but in a relationship. We are to be the hands and feet of Christ on earth.

"And I will make of you a great nation, and I will bless you and make your name great, so that you will be a blessing."

Genesis 12:2

Authentic Christians bless others. They recognize their mission and do the work they were created to do. They give and they serve others. They visit the lonely. They care for the broken hearted. They help the needy. They hear the voice of their shepherd and obey his command.

"Do not repay evil for evil or reviling for reviling, but on the contrary, bless, for to this you were called, that you may obtain a blessing."

1 Peter 3:9

Serving and giving is all about loving others as yourself. Real Christians know they have a calling to bless and to serve others. This is what makes them authentic Christians. So, let me ask you this; are you a real Christian or just a "sitting on the sidelines" Christian? Do you want to be a real Christian or are you comfortable leaving God's work for others to do? Are you too busy to serve the Lord?

All Christians have been called and commissioned! All Christians have been called to serve others!

So, when considering whether or not you are an authentic Christian, or just an unparticipating Christian, you can consider the kind of fruit that is produced in the life of a Christian.

"You did not choose me, but I chose you and appointed you so that you might go and bear fruit—fruit that will last—and so that whatever you ask in my name the 'Father' will give you."

John 15:16

Yes, even you! Jesus taught that we are given the tools to bear good fruit. Jesus says that the condition of a person's heart will determine what type of fruit we will produce.

"For no good tree bears bad fruit, nor again does a bad tree bear good fruit, for each tree is known by its own fruit. For figs are not gathered from thornbushes, nor are grapes picked from a bramble bush. The good person out of the good treasure of his heart produces good, and the evil person out of his evil treasure produces evil, for out of the abundance of the heart his mouth speaks.

Luke 6:43–45

The question is...Where is your fruit?

Are you serving God and bearing good fruit? Serving is one of the most important principles of the Christian faith, as believers are expected to help the church with a joyful spirit. "Love one another." "Care for one another." "Pray for one another." "Encourage one another." "Help one another." "Counsel one another." "Support one another." Scripture repeatedly tells us of our relationship to God and others through service.

You will recognize them by their fruits. Are grapes gathered from thornbushes, or figs from thistles?

Matthew 7:16

All Christians are called and equipped for the work of ministry, for building up the body of Christ. This is the very purpose for which we are created.

"For by grace you have been saved through faith. And this is not your own doing; it is the gift of God, not a result of works, so that no one may boast. For we are his workmanship, created in Christ Jesus for good works, which God prepared beforehand, that we should walk in them."

Ephesians 2:8–10

The Bible teaches that serving God and others is not about doing great things but about doing small things with great love. We can serve God and others daily by being kind to our neighbors, volunteering our time to help others, and giving to those in need.

We must remember that serving others may not always be easy, but God's grace and strength will help us. Secondly, we must remember that nothing is too small that God will not use it. Nothing we do for God is in vain!

"Teacher, which is the great commandment in the Law?" And he said to him, "You shall love the Lord your God with all your heart and with all your soul and with all your mind. This is the great and first commandment. And a second is like it: You shall love your neighbor as yourself. On these two commandments depend all the Law and the Prophets."

Matthew 22:36-40

How do we obey the greatest commandment? By Serving!

"Even as the Son of Man came not to be served but to serve, and to give his life as a ransom for many."

Matthew 20:28

Like Jesus, our purpose in life is to serve others! The core, central, primary characteristic of God . . . is love;

Anyone who does not love does not know God, because God is love.
1 John 4:8

If one is truly a hearer of the Word, then they will also be a doer of the Word. The only proper response to hearing the Word of God is by doing good works, it is in doing that the Word of God takes root. True faith is never alone, it always produces works.

Faith must lead to doing good works!

But what does it really mean to do "good works?" Here's a great definition we all should follow: A "good work" is *a righteous and biblically authorized action that is beneficial to others and for which God gets the glory and the credit."*

Only Christians can do good works!

Society has a different view of good works. They believe that if a person gives money to the poor, or some other worthy cause, that becomes a good work.

However, God sees things differently.

"Jesus looked up and saw the rich putting their gifts into the offering box, and he saw a poor widow put in two small copper coins. And he said, "Truly, I tell you, this poor widow has put in more than all of them. For they all contributed out of their abundance, but she out of her poverty put in all she had to live on."

Luke 21:1-4

Notice the difference? Good works are always a sacrifice, a secret, or something done to glorify God. Giving lots of money, even to a hospital, and having your name plastered on the building is glorifying yourself, not God. Sadly, even Christians do this, glorifying themselves, not God.

Then they said to him, "What must we do, to be doing the works of God?" Jesus answered them, "This is the work of God, that you believe in him whom he has sent."

John 6:28-29

Jesus says in John 6:28-29 that to do "good works" you must believe in Him (Jesus) whom the Father has sent. Again. Only Christians can truly do good works.

Look at this statement from Jesus;

Thus, when you give to the needy, sound no trumpet before you, as the hypocrites do in the synagogues and in the streets, that they may be praised by others. Truly, I say to you, they have received their reward. But when you give to the needy, do not let your left hand know what your right hand is doing, so that your giving may be in secret. And your 'Father' who sees in secret will reward you.

Matthew 6:2-4

When we serve and give to others, we are not to brag about it and boast about ourselves, we do it to glorify God. If we glorify ourselves, we are choosing to receive an award from people instead of receiving the reward from our Father. Serving and giving is done to glorify God, not ourselves.

We serve in obedience to God and we serve because we love God. Serving and giving is what Jesus did in his earthly mission and as followers of Jesus we must serve and love God and others.

Love is others focused with giving for the benefit of others. Love sacrifices self for the good of others.

Love comes from the character of God himself. All creation is designed by God with a principle giving and receiving. This is the secret on how life designed to function.

This giving and receiving is the key on which all creation was constructed to operate. Love is the principle of selfless giving, which is the foundation upon which all life is built to function. Simply put, love is the harmony of life. This created life design of God brings life, health and happiness.

Here is an example of how this giving and receiving is designed to work. The oceans give their waters to the clouds. The clouds then receive this water and gives rain on the earth. The earth receives this rain in water to form lakes, rivers and streams. The waters in lakes, rivers and streams in turn give these very waters to the plants and animals they need for survival. Then once again the plants and animals give the waters back to the ocean to start the same cycle all over again. It's clear God gives to us and we receive. After we receive, we must in turn give back. This completes the circle of life as designed by God.

Love is principle that sustains this cycle of life. If we fail to give after receiving, we break this circle of life. Timothy R. Jennings, M.D. in his book 'The God-Shaped Brain,' gives us some wonderful examples of how this principle works. Looking at the Dead Sea; the Dead Sea takes from the Jordan River but gives nothing in return. What happens in that body of water? The name says it all. Everything in the Dead Sea dies. Without giving everything stagnates and the cycle of life is broken.

Another example is in every breath we take. We receive oxygen and in turn we give away carbon dioxide to the plants, and the plants give back oxygen to us. Imagine if you were to decide, "I don't want to be a part of the circle of giving. If my body makes carbon dioxide, it's mine; I have the right to it. You can't have it." The only way to do that is to stop breathing—to die. If we hoard the product of our breathing, maybe by putting a bag over our heads, the carbon dioxide becomes the poisoning agent that kills us. In all life we see this circle of giving, which is the comes from the act of love.

The act of love is the design for all God's creation because all life flows from Him. Because God is love, He has written His law of love in all of nature because it is the design plan for life's basic operation.

Notice again how the circle of giving works in God's design.

The planets of our solar system circle around the sun, and the sun gives away its energy freely. Plants receive the sun's energy and, through metabolic "circles" internal to the plants (Calvin-Benson Cycle), convert the sun's energy into chemical energy. The plants give this energy to us in the form of fruits, nuts, grains, vegetables, and even oxygen to breathe. We receive the food from the plants and, through a series of metabolic "circles" internal to us (citric acid cycle), use the energy and convert the molecules to water, carbon dioxide and by products of digestion, which we give back to the earth, to fertilize the plants.

It's a never-ending circle of giving. In every living system, if it is to be healthy, the circle must not be broken. We see the circle of love in everything God created. The planets circle around the sun. The solar system circles in the galaxy, and the galaxies circle in the universe. Everything God creates gives freely in other-centered circles. It's no coincidence that when the prophet Ezekiel looked into heaven in a vision, what he saw symbolizing the foundation of God's government was a wheel within a wheel, a rotation within a rotation, a moving circle within a moving circle (Ezekeil 10:1-10).

God tried to teach us this basic truth within the Old Testament sacrificial system. In that system, a sinner would confess his sin on the head of an animal, and then the sinner would cut the animal's circulation. The life is in the blood (Leviticus 17:11), and it circles throughout the body.

The teaching is amazingly simple: sin severs the circle of life. The lifeblood of an animal is, naturally, its physical blood. The lifeblood of the economy is money; of an appliance, electricity. But the lifeblood of the universe is love, which flows from God through Christ to all creation and back to God through Christ again. This is God's design template. This is the blueprint on which humanity was created to operate! Whenever the circle of giving—the circle of love—is broken, pain, suffering and death inevitably follow. And it is only the love flowing from God that restores life, health and happiness.

Perhaps the most important application of this law is choosing to live in harmony with it. Because the law of love is the law of life, choosing to impart love to others is one of God's methods to strengthen you.

"Whoever brings blessing will be enriched, and one who waters will himself be watered."

Proverbs 11:25

Harmony with God's design promotes better health, here and now. Just as following the manufacturer's design protocol for your car and using unleaded gas rather than diesel results in more efficient function, so choosing to operate in harmony with God's design for life results in better mental and physical health. And scientific research demonstrates that, in fact, giving is living!

Dozens of studies over several decades have examined relationships between volunteer work and health-related outcomes. Most studies have shown positive volunteering-health associations.

Among youth, evidence suggests that volunteer work is associated with an excess of positive developmental outcomes, such as academic achievement, civic responsibility, and life skills that include leadership and interpersonal self-confidence (Astin & Sax 1998).

Four studies between 1996 and 2003 evaluated the effect of volunteerism and longevity in the elderly. Controlling for confounding variables, such as health when entering the study, all four studies "reported that volunteers tended to live statistically longer than those who did not volunteer. Not only do volunteers live longer but they live better too.

Just as the Bible teaches, ***to give is to live***. This is how God designed life to function. This is how God designed ***us*** to function! We will never function properly until we ***give***, until we ***serve*** others!

So why do so many, including myself, struggle to give?

"What good is it, my brothers, if someone says he has faith but does not have works? Can that faith save him? If a brother or sister is poorly clothed and lacking in daily food, and one of you says to them, "Go in peace, be warmed and filled," without giving them the things needed for the body, what good is that? So also, faith by itself, if it does not have works, is dead.

But someone will say, "You have faith and I have works." Show me your faith apart from your works, and I will show you my faith by my works. You believe that God is one; you do well. Even the demons believe—and shudder! Do you want to be shown, you foolish person, that faith apart from works is useless? Was not Abraham our father justified by works when he offered up his son Isaac on the altar? You see that faith was active along with his works, and faith was completed by his works; and the Scripture was fulfilled that says, "Abraham believed God, and it was counted to him as righteousness"—and he was called a friend of God. You see that a person is justified by works and not by faith alone. And in the same way was not also Rahab the prostitute justified by works when she received the messengers and sent them out by another way? For as the body apart from the spirit is dead, so also faith apart from works is dead."

James 2:14-26

Start serving and start living! 1

Don't be the kind of Christian who has an excuse not to give and serve. Don't say "God hasn't told me to serve." All believers have been called. It's clear in the Bible that all are called to serve. If you want to receive a blessing you need to serve. We are given gifts and blessings not for our benefit but for the benefit of others. Remember

TWO KINDS OF CHRISTIANS

a blessing is the God-given capacity to enjoy God's goodness in your life and to extend that goodness to others.

"It shall not be so among you. But whoever would be great among you must be your servant,"

Matthew 20:26

Are you the kind of Christian that is giving to and serving others, or are you the Christian that is only receiving from others?

THE CHRISTIAN WALK

"So that you will walk in a manner worthy of the Lord, to please Him in all respects, bearing fruit in every good work and increasing in the knowledge of God;"

Colossians 1:10

How is your Christian Walk and your relationship with Jesus Christ? Are you maturing in your walk? Are you growing? Are you maturing in your faith? Are you serving and giving?

These are the things we do as we grow in our Christian Walk.

As authentic Christians we grow day by day, we become more intimate with our savior, and we go deeper into the Word with greater understanding and clarity. We must be on a growth path to develop the spiritual traits an authentic Christian needs and desires to become a better Christian. As Max Lucado says, "God loves us where we are but He loves us too much to leave us there."

An authentic Christian knows we must always seek to grow in our faith and become better followers of Christ. We cannot be content to stay where we are. We desire growth and gaining more wisdom and knowledge because we desire a stronger relationship with our 'Father' and we realize that it only comes with spiritual maturity.

Are you following this path or are you happy where you are? Do you have a desire to grow and become more mature in your faith? If so ask yourself the following questions:

1. Are you walking in the light (1 John 1:4-7)?

2. Are you serious about sin and repentance (1 John 1:8-10)?

3. Do you desire to keep God's commands (1 John 2:3-4)?

4. Do you desire to walk as Christ walked (1 John 2:4-5)?

5. Do you have a disdain for the world and all that contradicts and opposes God's nature and will (1 John 2:15-17)?

6. Do you desire to have fellowship with other believers (1 John 2:18-19)?

7. Do you profess Christ to be God and hold Him in the highest esteem (1 John 2:22-24; 4:1-3, 13-15)?

8. Do you desire and long for the practical pursuit of holiness (1 John 3:1-3)?

9. Do you desire to practice righteousness (1 John 2:28-29; 3:4-10)?

10. Do you desire to overcome the world (1 John 4:4-6; 5:4-5)?

11. Do you pray regularly (1 Thessalonians 5:16-17)?

12. Do you believe the things that God has revealed concerning His Son, Jesus Christ, and believe you have eternal life in Him alone (1 John 5:9-12)?

If we have these qualities, and they are increasing in us, we have evidence that we have come to know God and bear the fruit of a child of God. We are maturing as we should be.

If these qualities are absent from our lives, we should have some concern for where we are in our Christian Walk. We should be diligent to seek God and we should reexamine ourselves to see if we are in the faith. We should be diligent to make our calling and election sure (2 Corinthians 13:5; 2 Peter 1:8-11).

For though by this time, you ought to be teachers, you need someone to teach you again the basic principles of the oracles of God. You need milk, not solid food, for everyone who lives on milk is unskilled in the word of righteousness, since he is a child. But solid food is for the mature, for those who have their powers of discernment trained by constant practice to distinguish good from evil.

Hebrews 5:12-14

Paul states here that the Christian Walk requires a constant growing and Christians go through various stages in their walk. Let's now look into these stages to gage if we are truly growing as we should.

Stages of the Christian Walk:

1. Spiritual Infant

This is the new believer. The new believer is in the stage of self-centeredness and still immature. We all start here and there is nothing wrong with this. This is where we start to grow and learn what it means to be a Christian. We get into the word and we learn more about God and his plan in the world and in our lives. We stay in this phase for a period of time but we must at some point start gaining some maturity so we can move on to the next phase of our Christian Walk.

"Like newborn babies, crave pure spiritual milk, so that by it you may grow up in your salvation, now that you have tasted that the Lord is good."

1 Peter 2:2-3

"Brothers and sisters, I could not address you as people who live by the Spirit but as people who are still worldly—mere infants in Christ. I

gave you milk, not solid food, for you were not yet ready for it. Indeed, you are still not ready. You are still worldly."

1 Corinthians 3:1-3

2. Spiritual Youth

You are now growing as a believer and learning.

"But solid food is for the mature, who by constant use have trained themselves to distinguish good from evil."

Hebrews 5:14

Spiritual growth is the norm, not the exception. Spiritual youth "are strong, and the word of God abides in them." As spiritual life flows, the body grows. This is why it is so important for every Christian to be closely connected to a local church. We grow in Christ as we are connected to a life-giving body. Spiritual youth are humble, teachable, and disciplined as they press on to full maturity in Christ.

3. Spiritual Parent

Now we are becoming mature believer and providers.

"And he gave the apostles, the prophets, the evangelists, the shepherds and teachers, to equip the saints for the work of ministry, for building up the body of Christ, until we all attain to the unity of the faith and of the knowledge of the Son of God, to mature manhood, to the measure of the stature of the fullness of Christ, so that we may no longer be children, tossed to and fro by the waves and carried about by every wind of doctrine, by human cunning, by craftiness in deceitful schemes. Rather, speaking the truth in love, we are to grow up in every way into him who is the head, into Christ."

Ephesians 4:11-15

Parents are knowledgeable and able to teach others. Parents become better skilled in the word of righteousness. Parents nurture and raise up others and become the witnesses of the faith. Parents aren't as focused on being feed but on feeding others. Parents are the servants and teachers in the local church. The church needs more spiritual parents. Without spiritual parents, a church can never be healthy. At this stage we should be participant in the church, not just sitting in attendance. We should be doing our part in the work of God's kingdom. We are still growing and learning but now our focus is more in helping others and bringing them into the knowledge of Christ. Not only are we now participating but we are now becoming leaders and teachers in the church. We give our time and talents to other and we are now focusing on others as we continue our Christian Walk.

4. Spiritual Mentor

In this stage we become true disciples and fishers of men.

"Go therefore and make disciples of all nations, baptizing them in the name of the Father and of the Son and of the Holy Spirit, teaching them to observe all that I have commanded you. And behold, I am with you always, to the end of the age."

Matthew 28:19-20

Mentors are fishing for men and women who will themselves become fishers of men and women. We move from teaching others into training others to be teachers. The goal of discipleship is to help people follow Jesus who will then become teachers of others on how to follow Jesus enabling them to become the disciples of others in how to follow Jesus. As believers grow into the final stage of Christian maturity, they become disciples and mentors. Discipleship involves learning from Jesus, following His teachings, and applying them to daily life. As Christians, we are to follow Jesus' example by demonstrating His love toward one another and putting other's needs before our own. As mentors we are to call our students into doing what Jesus did. Our students then go into the world to become a disciple who makes other disciples.

"If I then, your Lord and Teacher, have washed your feet, you also ought to wash one another's feet. For I have given you an example, that you also should do just as I have done to you. Truly, truly, I say to you, a servant is not greater than his master, nor is a

messenger greater than the one who sent him. If you know these things, blessed are you if you do them."

John 13:14-17

"To this you were called, because Christ suffered for you, leaving you an example, that you should follow in his steps."

1 Peter 2:21

Are you the kind of Christian that is mature in your Christian walk, or the Christian that is still struggling with immaturity?

ASSURED SALVATION

"You will be hated by everyone because of me, but the one who stands firm to the end will be saved."

Matthew 10:22

So now to the big question, how do we know that we are truly saved?

The parable of the sower may be a good place to start:

"Again, he began to teach beside the sea. And a very large crowd gathered about him, so that he got into a boat and sat in it on the sea, and the whole crowd was beside the sea on the land. And he was teaching them many things in parables, and in his teaching, he said to them: "Listen! Behold, a sower went out to sow. And as he sowed, some seed fell along the path, and the birds came and devoured it. Other seed fell on rocky ground, where it did not have much soil, and immediately it sprang up, since it had no depth of soil. And when the sun rose, it was scorched, and since it had no root, it withered away. Other seed fell among thorns, and the thorns grew up and choked it, and it yielded no grain. And other seeds fell into good soil and produced grain, growing up and increasing and yielding thirtyfold and sixtyfold and a hundredfold." And he said, "He who has ears to hear, let him hear." And when he was alone, those around him with the twelve asked him about the parables. And he said to them, "To you has been given the secret of the kingdom of God, but for those outside everything is in parables, so that "'they may indeed see but not

perceive, and may indeed hear but not understand, lest they should turn and be forgiven.'" And he said to them, "Do you not understand this parable? How then will you understand all the parables? The sower sows the word. And these are the ones along the path, where the word is sown: when they hear, Satan immediately comes and takes away the word that is sown in them. And these are the ones sown on rocky ground: the ones who, when they hear the word, immediately receive it with joy. And they have no root in themselves, but endure for a while; then, when tribulation or persecution arises on account of the word, immediately they fall away. And others are the ones sown among thorns. They are those who hear the word, but the cares of the world and the deceitfulness of riches and the desires for other things enter in and choke the word, and it proves unfruitful. But those that were **sown on the good soil** *are the ones who* **hear the word and accept it** *and* **bear fruit**, *thirtyfold and sixtyfold and a hundredfold."*

Mark 4:1-20

There are four types of soils found in this parable: one that flat-out rejects Christianity, two that seem to be interested in Christianity but don't prove genuine (they are distracted by the cares of the world or disinterested after hardship), and one "good" soil that truly believes and bears fruit for Christ. Just like the fruitless seed that fell upon rocky and thorny ground, there are Christians who hear the Word of God and attend church regularly who do not show the signs of being saved and are not genuinely converted. So just by looking at this one parable, we see four requirements needed to be saved. These four requirements can be formed ask questions you can ask yourself:

1. **Are you planted on good soil?**
   We all need to examine ourselves to confirm that God is working in our hearts as believers.
   - Do you believe Jesus Christ is God?
   - Do you submit to Jesus as your Lord and Savior?
   - Do you trust Jesus alone for salvation?
   - Have you put your faith in Jesus and not idols?

- Is Jesus your cornerstone?
- Are you standing firm on solid ground?

2. Do you hear the word and understand it?
- Are you spending time in the bible?
- Do you understand the Bible?
- Do you rely on the Holy Spirit for understanding?

3. Do you accept the word?
- Do you love God?
- Do you love people?
- Do you obey what God says in the bible?
- Do you love Jesus and want to please Him?
- Have you repented of your sins?
- Are you truly shamed and sorry for your sin?
- Are you trusting God to forgive your sins?
- Are you sinning less and less?
- Do you believe in the promises of God?
- Do you put all your faith and trust in Jesus?
- Do you believe in your heart, not just your head?
- Do you believe that God keeps His promises!

4. Do you bear fruit?
- Is the fruit of the Spirit increasing in your life?
- Do you serve other believers?
- Do you serve unbelievers?
- Do you pray with others?

Obviously, we should all have answered "Yes" to these questions. Every one of the statements describes the pattern of life for an authentic Christian. Yet biblically, no Christian is absolutely good or righteous in ourselves. Christians still sin, even though Romans 5:1 says that an authentic Christian is justified by faith in Christ. Justification means the person has been declared to be righteous.

"For our sake he made him to be sin who knew no sin, so that in him we might become the righteousness of God."

2 Corinthians 5:21

We could say a spiritually maturing Christian is someone who seeks to please God in everything they do in action, word, thought and motive (1 Thessalonians 4:1). They will strive to flee sin, read the Bible, pray, be filled with the Holy Spirit, confess their sins and share Christ with others.

The Bible is clear that when someone is saved, the new creation they become will be evident by a change in lifestyle. A true, born-again Christian will strive to bring glory and honor to Christ by living a life that is pleasing to God (1 Peter 1:15–16). True saving faith will always be evidenced by the fruit of the Spirit that lives in the heart. The "false Christian" doesn't have the ability to produce the Spirit's fruit and continues to exhibit the works of the flesh (Galatians 5:19–26). As Jesus reminded His disciples, we know who they are by their fruits (Matthew 7:20). Therefore, any profession of faith that does not result in a changed life and fruit of the Spirit is a false profession, and the professor is not a Christian. 1

"For by grace you have been saved through faith. And this is not your own doing; it is the gift of God, not a result of works, so that no one may boast."

Ephesians 2:8-9

If you want to dig a little deeper into understanding your salvation, I suggest you read the book of 1st John. This book can serve as something like a test to examine ourselves and our faith. As we look at the twelve highlights below, please remember that no one will perfectly fulfill all of these examples all the time, but they should reveal a consistent trend that characterizes our lives as we grow in grace.

1. Do you enjoy having fellowship with Christ and His redeemed people? (1 John 1:3)

2. Would people say you walk in the light, or walk in the darkness? (1 John 1:6-7)

3. Do you admit and confess your sin? (1 John 1:8)

4. Are you obedient to God's Word? (1 John 2:3-5)

5. Does your life indicate you love God rather than the world? (1 John 2:15)

6. Is your life characterized by "doing what is right"? (1 John 2:29)

7. Do you seek to maintain a pure life? (1 John 3:3)

8. Do you see a decreasing pattern of sin in your life? (1 John 3:5-6)

9. Do you demonstrate love for other Christians? (1 John 3:14)

10. Do you "walk the walk," versus just "talking the talk"? (1 John 3:18-19)

11. Do you maintain a clear conscience? (1 John 3:21)

12. Do you experience victory in your Christian Walk? (1 John 5:4)

Yes, these two lists have some of the same questions, however these two lists verify that there is no need to doubt your salvation when you answer yes to these questions. These questions can demonstrate if your life is bearing the fruit of true salvation. If you're not there yet don't despair. Now you have a target to aim for and you will hit this target if you trust in the Lord to get you there.

Jesus said that it is by our fruits that we are known as His disciples (Matthew 7:20). Fruitless branches—professing believers who do not display the fruit of the Spirit (Galatians 5:22-23) are cut off and thrown into the fire (John 15:6). A genuine faith is one that not only believes in God (the demons themselves do that - James 2:19), but leads to open confession of sin and obedience to Christ's commands. Remember, we are saved by grace through faith, not by our works (Ephesians 2:8-9), but our works should display the reality of our salvation (James 2:17-18). Genuine saving faith will always produce works.

In addition to these confirmations, we need to remember God's promises and the reality of the war we are in. Satan is just as real as Jesus Christ, and he is a formidable enemy of our souls. When we turn to Christ, Satan will look for every opportunity to deceive and defeat us. He will try to convince us that we are unworthy failures or that God has given up on us. When we are in Christ, we have the assurance that we are kept by Him. Jesus Himself prayed for us saying;

"And I am no longer in the world, but they are in the world, and I am coming to you. Holy Father, keep them in your name, which you have given me, that they may be one, even as we are one."

John 17:11

Again, in verse 15, Jesus prayed,

"I do not ask that you take them out of the world, but that you keep them from the evil one."

John 17:15

One of the oldest tricks of the devil is to make Christians doubt their salvation. When we doubt our salvation, we doubt God's Word, and when we doubt God's Word, we are powerless and ineffective tools for Christ. Jesus also said;

"My sheep hear my voice, and I know them, and they follow me. I give them eternal life, and they will never perish, and no one will snatch them out of my hand. My Father, who has given them to me, is greater than all, and no one is able to snatch them out of the Father's hand."

John 10:27-29

If you hear and obey the voice of Jesus, then you are one of His sheep, and He will never let you go. Jesus gave a wonderful word picture here of Christians securely held within His loving hands and the Father's almighty hands wrapping themselves around His, giving us a double assurance of eternal security. 2

A lot of people believe they are saved only if they have some powerful emotion or overwhelming feeling. However, every Christian has times when feelings are not strong, no matter what our experiences may have been in the past. But it is not our feelings that save us—it is Christ.

"How can we know we are really saved? Because God's Word tells us, and God cannot lie. If you have put your personal sincere faith and trust in Jesus Christ as your Lord and Savior, the Bible says God has made you a member of His family.

"And this is the testimony, that God gave us eternal life, and this life is in his Son. Whoever has the Son has life; whoever does not have the Son of God does not have life."

1 John 5:11-13

As someone once said, 'God said it—I believe it—that settles it!'

"Remember that God loves you. And if you begin to doubt, remember the promises He has made to you and the way He loves you. Learn to thank Him for that love. When we know Christ, nothing 'shall be able to separate us from the love of God, which is in Christ Jesus our Lord' (Romans 8:39)."

When Jesus died on the cross, He declared "it is finished" because He paid the price in full. The path to salvation for anyone who will repent has been laid out. He declared it was finished because there was nothing else that could be done. All someone had to do moving forward to spend eternity with the Lord is to repent of their sins, so they can be washed in the blood of Jesus, and begin a relationship with God, unencumbered by their sins. After the moment of belief, repentance, and acceptance, the Holy Spirit fills them, and they are sealed by the Spirit until Jesus' return.

Jesus Himself assures those who believe in Him:

"I give them eternal life, and they will never perish, and no one will snatch them out of my hand. My Father, who has given them to me, is greater than all, and no one is able to snatch them out of the Father's hand."

John 10:28–29

Eternal life is just that—eternal. There is no one, not even yourself, who can take Christ's God-given gift of salvation away from you.

Take joy in what God's Word is saying to you: instead of doubting, we can live with confidence! We can have the assurance from Christ's own Word that our salvation will never be in question. Our assurance of salvation is based on the perfect and complete salvation God has provided for us through Jesus Christ. Are you sincerely trusting in the Lord Jesus Christ as your Savior? If the answer is "yes," rest assured, you are saved.

What kind of Christian are you?

The Christian that is sure of you salvation...or,

The Christian who is NOT sure of your salvation?

Be sure of your salvation today. Confess your sins to God, repent of your sins to God, and receive Jesus as your Lord and Savior. For it is with your heart that you believe and are justified. When you do this with sincerity of heart, then you will know, without a doubt, that you are truly saved.

Take this step now!

Become the kind of Christian that is truly saved.

CONCLUSION

"As for the promise which I made you when you came out of Egypt, My Spirit is abiding in your midst; do not fear!"

Haggai 2:5

There are no specific rituals that make someone a Christian. Being a Christian involves thanking God through your efforts and sharing his compassion and love with others in this dark world. These efforts may include many things like inviting people to church, working for justice, donating blood, providing hospitality, tutoring a child, welcoming a newcomer, or volunteering for community services. One must act like a Christian with true intentions. It's the heart's condition that counts, and not just the act itself.

If you call yourself a Christian, what can I depend on you to do?

Oddly, the term Christian is not part of Jesus' instructions to his disciples. He doesn't mention the term at all. The word 'Christian' was a descriptive term applied to the disciples of Jesus by the non-Christians in Antioch. It was meant as an insult, not a compliment. The followers of Jesus seem to have gradually accepted the term. The term 'Christian' simply means that you are a disciple of Jesus Christ.

Anyone can come to Jesus and call themselves a Christian. And, when they do, Christ takes a personal interest in them. To whatever extent one actually believes Jesus and acts on the things Jesus said, their life is made better. The Holy Spirit will begin to work in your life.

Being an authentic Christian involves both beliefs and actions.

Believing that God actually exists is obviously the starting point. One cannot be a Christian if he or she doesn't first believe in an invisible power that created everything (Genesis 1:1; 2:4). It is essential that a true Christian will believe in a Supreme Being of superior power and intellect who is responsible for all life. You cannot be a Christian and deny that God is responsible for the creation of the universe and all life.

Authentic Christians believe Jesus Christ was God in the flesh.

Christianity is based on Jesus Christ. Christians believe He did exist and walked the roads of Judea about 2,000 years ago. But it isn't enough to believe simply that the historical figure Jesus Christ lived. An authentic Christian must believe Jesus is who He said He was—the Son of God. He was God. He was the Word (the being who communicated with mankind in the Old Testament), who came to earth as a human being (John 1:1-3, 14; Philippians 2:5-8).

Authentic Christians believe Christ died for the sins of all humanity and was resurrected to eternal life.

"Behold! The Lamb of God who takes away the sin of the world!"
John 1:29

This statement from John the Baptist sums up the Christian belief.

"So, Christ, having been offered once to bear the sins of many, will appear a second time, not to deal with sin but to save those who are eagerly waiting for him."
Hebrews 9:28

But if Jesus had stayed dead, we would still be in our sins and not have a living Savior.

"For if the dead are not raised, not even Christ has been raised. And if Christ has not been raised, your faith is futile and you are still in your sins. Then those also who have fallen asleep in Christ have perished. If in Christ we have hope in this life only, we are of all people most to be pitied. But in fact, Christ has been raised from the dead, the first fruits of those who have fallen asleep."

1 Corinthians 15:16-20

Thankfully, on the third day, Jesus was resurrected to life again by the Father (Matthew 12:40). He is alive today and seated at the right hand of His Father in heaven (Hebrews 12:2). We have a living Savior and an eternal hope.

Authentic Christians are characterized by having love for one another and the eternal hope that is present. Hope is a vital mainstay of the Christian life unlike in other religions or in our secular society. The world lacks hope. For them this life offers the last opportunity for hope. Those without faith in Christ will one day be without hope. In the famous writing by Dante Alighieri, 'Divine Comedy,' inscribed above the entrance of the gates of Hell is the statement, "For those who are about to enter, abandon all hope."

What a horrible reality lies ahead for those who are far away from God. If this is you, please evaluate where you are now and discover the true hope that can be yours today in Christ Jesus.

Only Christians have this hope. It is vitally important to receive Jesus as your Lord and Savor through faith in Him. You only have this one life to decide because after this life is finished, there will be no more hope. Take this opportunity now to receive the free gift of salvation that is only available through Jesus Christ. Put your faith in Him right now! Become a true follower of Jesus so you can have a lasting hope.

Jesus Christ made this crucial statement identifying His followers:

"By this all will know that you are My disciples, if you have love for one another."

John 13:35

Love and outward concern for others, should be a key trait of every Christian. Love is so important, a whole chapter in the Bible is dedicated to explaining what it looks like in action.

*If I speak in the tongues of men and of angels, but have not **love**, I am a noisy gong or a clanging cymbal. And if I have prophetic powers, and understand all mysteries and all knowledge, and if I have all faith, so as to remove mountains, but have not **love**, I am nothing. If I give away all I have, and if I deliver up my body to be burned, but have not **love**, I gain nothing. **Love** is patient and kind; **love** does not envy or boast; it is not arrogant or rude. It does not insist on its own way; it is not irritable or resentful; it does not rejoice at wrongdoing, but rejoices with the truth. **Love** bears all things, believes all things, hopes all things, endures all things. **Love never ends**. As for prophecies, they will pass away; as for tongues, they will cease; as for knowledge, it will pass away. For we know in part and we prophesy in part, but when the perfect comes, the partial will pass away. When I was a child, I spoke like a child, I thought like a child, I reasoned like a child. When I became a man, I gave up childish ways. For now, we see in a mirror dimly, but then face to face. Now I know in part; then I shall know fully, even as I have been fully known. So now faith, hope, and **love** abide, these three; **but the greatest of these is love**.*

1 Corinthians 13.

Love simply cannot be overlooked. It is the nature of God and as we are created in God's image, it must also be our nature if we are true believers.

As real Christians, we must believe that the entire Bible is the inspired Word of God. There is a misconception among many that the Old Testament is a mix of fictional stories and boring old laws with very little relevance today. Over the years, various polls show that the percentage of people who believe that the whole Bible is the inspired Word of God is declining.

Real Christians believe the Bible is exactly what it says it is—the inspired Word of God.

Real Christians take what the Bible says seriously, respect what it says, and strives to live by its words.

"All these things my hand has made, and so all these things came to be, declares the Lord. But this is the one to whom I will look: he who is humble and contrite in spirit and trembles at my word."

Isaiah 66:2

The Bible declares that;

"All Scripture is breathed out by God and profitable for teaching, for reproof, for correction, and for training in righteousness, that the man of God may be complete, equipped for every good work."

2 Timothy 3:16-17

As Christians we believe we are saved by our faith, and good works are a by-product of our faith. There are many people who believe they are "saved," but live a life that is anything but Christian. Many believe, contrary to the Bible, that God basically requires only a belief in Him and His Son's sacrifice. As we saw above, this is essential. But real Christians understand that belief and faith also lead ultimately to something more, it must lead to a sincere love for God and for others with a commitment to also serving God and others.

We understand that salvation is a free gift of God's grace and it can never be earned. If it has to be earned, then it really isn't a free gift. But we must also look carefully to biblical instruction that joins faith and good works.

But someone will say, "You have faith and I have works." Show me your faith apart from your works, and I will show you my faith by my works.

James 2:18

God's Ten Commandments are the basis for the good works an authentic Christian does. Belief and faith cannot be separated from works of righteousness. They are linked and mutually dependent on each other. Because of our faith and belief, we commit our lives to obedience to God and doing good works. Instead of viewing the Ten Commandments as abolished or irrelevant, real Christians view them as their guide to living a righteous life. Open you Bible and read the Ten Commandments now (Exodus 20). You will see that all ten commandments point to loving God, and loving people. That's it! That's what the Christian life is all about. ***LOVE!***

If you can love, you can easily become a Christian.

Authentic Christians strive to dramatically change their lives. Unfortunately, there are many polls that have shown that the majority of professing Christians do not live a lifestyle much different from that of non-Christians. Many Christian churches talk about "giving your heart to the Lord" and coming to God "just as you are"— but neglect the full biblical definition of being converted. One of the clearest definitions of Christian conversion is found below;

"To put off your old self, which belongs to your former manner of life and is corrupt through deceitful desires, and to be renewed in the spirit of your minds, and to put on the new self, created after the likeness of God in true righteousness and holiness."

Ephesians 4:22-24

This passage describes a total transformation of one's life. Becoming the 'New Creation", we discussed earlier. This involves leaving our old sinful ways of thinking and acting, and instead living an entirely new way of life—a way of life defined by "righteousness and holiness."

Authentic Christianity is not just a professing belief in Jesus or being a member in a church—it is an entire transformation of our mind and conduct.

"Do not be conformed to this world, but be transformed by the renewal of your mind, that by testing you may discern what is the will of God, what is good and acceptable and perfect."

Romans 12:2

The real Christian is an individual that is striving to follow and imitate Jesus Christ's example in every aspect of their life. Have you found areas where your beliefs don't reflect true biblical Christianity? If so, it's not too late to change. Are you ready to dedicate your life to becoming a true Christian? If so, just focus on the following points:

1. Believe that you are loved and accepted by God.

The good news of the Christian faith begins with the recognition that you are loved and accepted by the God who created and sustains the world. Jesus taught us to call God "Father." While some people may lack the positive experience of a loving parent, most can imagine what the word "father" can mean at its very best. It suggests one who gives life, supplies love, provides care, protects, guides, watches over, enables growth, and gives freedom. This is what God is like. Even when we do not acknowledge God, God cares for us like a mother who cares for her children. God knows us intimately and loves us totally. Nothing we have done or could do can make God love us less.

2. Admit that you are a sinner.

The Bible plainly teaches that every human being has sinned, and has lost the desire to serve God, and has no ability to save themselves. We see this truth in the realization that human failures, wrong choices, and stubborn self-will leave us guilty and powerless, and that habits can easily become addictions that are almost impossible to break. Not only that, but human sin affects our whole society, creating a world full of injustice, greed, oppression, pornography, pollution, and violence. Despite this sinfulness, God did not stop loving us or desiring fellowship with us. As strange as this may seem to us, we are taught that;

"God so loved the world that he gave his only Son, so that everyone who believes in him may not perish but may have eternal life."

John 3:16

Through the life, death, and resurrection of Jesus, we gain the right to become daughters and sons of God and receive the sure hope that this new life will continue beyond death, bringing us into heaven. That's the good news of the Christian faith!

3. Acknowledge and repent of your sins.

It's not enough to admit that you have sinned. You must regret those sins, and then turn away from them. The New Testament uses several words to describe a genuine response to the gospel message. The first word is "repentance," which in the original Greek literally means "turn around" or "change of mind." We are told it is a crucial part of responding to the good news of God's grace. When you hear the word "repentance," you may think immediately of feeling or being sorry. Being sorry is appropriate, but it's not the main sense of the word "repentance" at all. Repentance involves a change in your thinking and in your actions. Your will and your behavior will also change. True repentance means that you want to please God rather than yourself. You come to love what is good, not what is bad. You experience a life directed outwardly to connect with others, rather than inwardly focused on yourself.

4. Commit your life to Christ.

Faith is another key word the New Testament uses to describe a genuine response to the good news. Accept what God has done by faith and receive salvation as a gift. And in response, commit your life to following Christ, and enter into a relationship with Him through prayer, Bible reading, and worship. We come to know and love God more through the Holy Spirit, who enters our hearts. Once we have committed our lives to Christ, the Holy Spirit lives and works within us. "When the Spirit of truth comes," said Jesus in John 16:13-14, "He will guide you into all the truth...He will take what is mine and declare it to you." It is not important how we come to Christ, but that we do come to Christ.

5. Live a life of gratitude to God.

Christian living involves a transformation of our lives out of gratitude to God. Obedience to God in the Ten Commandments is seen as an opportunity to express thanks to God for what God has done. Obedience is not seen as a means of winning approval, but of showing love and appreciation to God. Jesus taught his disciples, "If you love me, you will keep my commandments" (John 14:15). This understanding of life as gratitude has two important consequences. First, it frees us from continual concern about our performance. We do not need to keep asking "Am I good enough?" because our purpose is simply to let our lives express our joy and gratitude. Second, all of life is now seen as an opportunity to serve God. We also express our gratitude through the way we treat our family and friends, perform our jobs, use our leisure time, vote, and participate in community. bear witness to our faith. We say thanks to God through all our efforts to share his love and compassion with the world. As true Christians, we show our love for God by the way we relate to others. [1]

"Beloved, since God loved us so much, we also ought to love one another.

1 John 4:11

There is a God, and you are made in His image. This means you have value. Christians have a source of real love since God made us in His loving image. As Christians, we have a solid foundation for knowing there is right and wrong because God's laws are written in our hearts. Jesus Christ, who is God the Son, loved you enough to come down and die in your place so we can experience God's goodness and love for all eternity.

The day is coming when we all will give an account before God for our actions and thoughts. Will you repent, change your mind, change your actions, and receive Christ as your Lord and Savior today so that you will join Christ in eternity?

Our God is humble and loving. This is what God, in the form and person of Jesus did for us.

"Though He was God, He did not think of equality with God as something to cling to. Instead, He gave up his divine privileges; He took the humble position of a slave and was born as a human being. When He appeared in human form, He humbled himself in obedience to God and died a criminal's death on a cross. Therefore, God elevated Him to the place of highest honor and gave Him the name above all other names, that at the name of Jesus every knee should bow, in Heaven and on earth and under the earth, and every tongue declare that Jesus Christ is Lord, to the glory of God the Father."

Philippians 2:6-11

If all the people of this world could only comprehend how much God truly loves them, they would all be eager to get to know Him.

How about you?

Would you like to get to know the true loving and Living God? The creator of the universe.

He's waiting for you with all His love!

What you can gain is unimaginable!

What do you have to lose?

REFERENCES

INTRODUCTION
1. https://www.compellingtruth.org/fake-Christians.html

LOVING THE WORLD
1. https://www.gotquestions.org/do-not-love-the-world.html

LOVING GOD
1. https://www.gotquestions.org/Bible-self-examination.html
2. https://www.desiringgod.org/interviews/how-do-i-live-the-authentic-christian-life
3. https://www.neverthirsty.org/seeking-god/marks-of-a-christian/self-inventory-test/

LOVING THE CHURCH
1. https://www.ligonier.org/learn/articles/what-church
2. https://www.christianity.com/church/what-is-the-church-its-purpose-and-identity.html
3. https://www.christianity.com/church/what-is-the-church-its-purpose-and-identity.html

LOVING OTHERS
1. https://www.desiringgod.org/messages/the-link-between-gods-love-for-us-and-ours-for-others
2. https://www.desiringgod.org/articles/three-lessons-on-loving-one-another
3. https://www.aol.com/gates-police-looking-satanic-graffiti-142927275.html

4. https://nonprofitssource.com/online-giving-statistics/church-giving/
5. https://christianeducatorsacademy.com/how-to-have-a-good-heart-as-a-christian-7-key-ways/#:~:text=Simply%20put%2C%20it%20means%20having%20a%20heart%20that,seeking%20to%20serve%20others%2C%20just%20as%20Christ%20did.
6. https://www.gotquestions.org/Bible-compassion.html
7. https://www.compellingtruth.org/Bible-compassion.html
8. https://seekinggodwithjoy.com/practical-compassion-how-everyday-compassion-makes-us-more-like-jesus-tips/
9. https://bible.org/article/rescue-why-did-jesus-come
10. https://www.gotquestions.org/Jesus-mission.html
11. https://www.rlhymersjr.com/Online_Sermons/2007/062407PM_SeekSalvationOfTheLost.html
12. https://www.ligonier.org/learn/devotionals/seeking-and-saving-lost

GLORIFYING GOD

1. https://www.gotquestions.org/glorify-God.html
2. https://www.desiringgod.org/messages/glorifying-god-period

BECOMING LIKE JESUS

1. https://www.desiringgod.org/articles/three-lessons-on-loving-one-another
2. https://www.womanofnoblecharacter.com/ways-to-become-more-like-christ/

BECOMING A NEW CREATION

1. https://preachitteachit.org/ask_roger/are-christians-really-that-judgmental/
2. https://www.christianity.com/wiki/sin/why-is-sin-used-to-self-righteously-judge-others.html
3. https://relevantmagazine.com/faith/why-are-christians-so-judgmental/
4. https://www.cru.org/us/en/how-to-know-god/what-is-a-christian.html

5. https://billygraham.org/answer/why-is-forgiving-others-important/

6. https://www.ligonier.org/learn/articles/what-does-it-mean-to-forgive

7. https://christian.net/videos/bible-stories/what-does-it-mean-to-be-a-new-creation-in-christ-jesus/#:~:text=A%20New%20Purpose%20and%20Calling%3A%20As%20a%20new,a%20way%20that%20reflects%20the%20character%20of%20Christ.

NEW PRIORITIES

1. https://lifehopeandtruth.com/change/christian-conversion/christian-priorities/

2. https://bible.org/seriespage/lesson-9-priorities-god-s-people-1-peter-24-10

DISCOVERING YOUR PURPOSE

1. https://halyministries.com/how-to-live-a-life-of-purpose-as-a-christian-7-keys-to-discovering-your-god-given-calling/#:~:text=Living%20purposefully%20as%20a%20Christian%20means%20pursuing%20God%E2%80%99s,seek%20wise%20counsel%2C%20and%20step%20out%20in%20faith.

ABANDONING YOUR COMFORT ZONE

1. https://applygodsword.com/what-does-the-bible-say-about-leaving-your-comfort-zone/

SERVING AND GIVING

1. Jennings, Timothy R. Jennings, M.D. The God-Shaped Brain: How Changing Your View of God Transforms Your Life. InterVarsity Press. Kindle Edition.

THE CHRISTIAN WALK

N/A

ASSURED SALVATION

1. https://billygraham.org/answer/i-dont-always-feel-saved-how-can-i-be-sure-i-am/

2. https://www.gotquestions.org/signs-saving-faith.html

CONCLUSION

1. https://www.faithward.org/how-do-you-become-a-christian/

Made in the USA
Columbia, SC
02 January 2025

50944154R00114